Amazon FBA

A Step-by-Step Guide on Creating Your First Money Making Online Business from the Comfort of Your Own Home! Crush your competitor's Launches and Sell your Winning products!

By Kiyo Richards

TABLE OF CONTENTS

Chapter 1: Introduction to Amazon FBA 1

Chapter 2: Basic overview of FBA and signing up .. 18

Chapter 3: Mastering Amazon Algorithm techniques 32

Chapter 4: Negotiation with Alibaba suppliers 52

Chapter 5: Keyword Research for FBA 64

Chapter 6: Tips for the fast shipping process 80

Chapter 7: Advanced marketing strategies to drive sales 91

Chapter 8: How to find profitable products? 111

Chapter 9: Getting rid of Project hijackers 127

Chapter 10: Roadmap to private labelled products 141

Introduction

Congratulations on purchasing *Amazon FBA* and thank you for doing so.

The following chapters will discuss various topics related to the Amazon fulfillment business model in detail. Apply these techniques in the real world to get fruitful results.

There are plenty of books on this subject on the market, thanks again for choosing this one! Every effort was made to ensure it is full of as much useful information as possible, please enjoy it!

Chapter 1: Introduction to Amazon FBA

Before going to start talking about the fundamentals of Amazon FBA business, we need to understand the basics of e-commerce businesses that have evolved into a successful and convenient business model and offered a lot of scope for future enterprises to reduce the impact of traditional motor brick industries.

What is an e-commerce business?

Before the era of the internet, wholesale marketers are the rulers of the industrial supply. Starting from the industrial revolution that has evolved in the mid-1850s with the export and import of spices there is no hurdle for mortar and brick industries who delivered products to the shops directly for the customers who would come to the shops to buy whatever they need.

This chain of mechanism has made good profits for the suppliers and has become a burden for sellers due to fluctuations in prices depending on various factors. However, in the early 2000s internet has boomed making businesses thrive. Years passed and the Internet has become a necessity making new enterprises evolve with time. One of those days, Amazon has become live on the internet and it never looked back since then.

What is the Amazon business model?

Amazon acts as an intermediary between the seller and buyer using its websites or apps. A buyer can digitally order the products and receive the product within a minor frame with the help of amazon's efficient logistics supply. Moreover, Amazon prefers and gives importance to customer's satisfaction more than any factor thus making people coming back to it for every need so often.

However, Amazon does not sell everything in its platform unlike other millions of private stores that offer various niche products for its visitors. Amazon collaborated with lakhs of business supplies also called sellers into a complex network system with its efficient logistics system to deliver products to the buyers.

What is Amazon FBA in brief?

Amazon FBA in layman terms is defined as Fulfilled by Amazon. This technically describes that the seller can use amazon's efficient logistic support to deliver the products, unlike Amazon FBM where the seller needs to ship the products to the buyer by himself.

Are you still in confusion about how Amazon FBA works? Head over and read the systematic procedure that explains the process that goes on with the famous Amazon fulfillment service.

The working steps of Amazon FBA

1) First of all, the Amazon seller needs to send his products in a neatly packed procedure according to the amazon standards to one of its warehouses that are situated in almost every part of the country.

2) When the product is received by the Amazon warehouse the listing goes live on the website and customers can order the products. Received product is stored in those well-established warehouses until the product gets ordered by the buyer.

3) Amazon is responsible for any mishaps that may happen to the products inside the warehouses. Amazon has a strict policy to reimburse any damaged product money to the sellers due to the mistake of its logistics department.

4) When the product is ordered by a customer amazon packs it to the customer and sends it to the shipping address all by its own by its well-established delivery department or by its sibling delivery partners.

5) All the while amazon is responsible for any delivery delay or wrong product delivery to the customers and the sellers need not worry about the customer assistance that they otherwise need to do on their own or by third party call services.

6) If a buyer is not satisfied with the product, he may raise a return ticket that will be fulfilled by the Amazon. After the end of the return policy timeframe, the seller will receive his funds excluding the basic amazon Fulfilment service fees in his bank account.

This is the basic structure of the business model that goes on when you are partnered with Amazon fulfillment service. I hope that clears away your thoughts about the basic process. In the next section, we will describe the things that sellers should follow in this business model. Let us go!

What sellers should be aware of?

1) Choosing the right product

If you are serious about making money with amazon, then you need to find the right product to sell. Choosing to sell some mediocre or unpopular products may land you into losses. If you can get one unique product that can attract consumers of your niche your business will grow very easily. Therefore, in this book, we will discuss various strategies that can help you choose the right product. We will also go through the concept of private label products that is a successful strategy to earn more profits using Amazon FBA.

2) Keyword research

Amazon algorithm works on the basic principle of keywords. Whenever you try to create a listing, the system asks you to insert a few mandatory keywords so that the user can see your product in his search results. There are many ways to find successful and profitable keywords with very little competition. You can simply use the amazon default search recommendations to get an overall estimation of popular products. However, to get good profitable results using Amazon FBA the sellers need to get accustomed to keyword tools like keyword tool.io, amazon jungle scout that displays the competitive strength in their results. We will discuss various keyword strategies in detail in the coming chapters.

3) Negotiating with partners

People often get confused with the significant terms of drop shipping and amazon fulfillment. Dropshipping is the process where you just act like a middleman and sell the products from the retailers to the consumers. You need not worry about manufacturing, shipping and any other parameters that come with it.

However, there is no way that you can know about the quality of the product and you may land in losses if the customers start retiring the product due to varied reasons. In a word, if you are a drop shipper there are very fewer things that you can control and all you can do is believe with all guts about your supplier. This is the reason why there are very few successful drop-shippers in the industry.

Amazon FBA covers these disadvantages that dropshipping provides with the power of controlling things on your own excluding the logistic department.

However, when trying to expand your business using Amazon FBA or while giving inputs for retailers to create private-labelled products you need to negotiate with them for reducing the costs. A lot of wholesale retailers and manufacturers are available through websites like Alibaba that belong to China. For this reason, every Amazon FBA seller should improve his negotiation skills with the manufacturers for more profits. In the later chapters, we will discuss different strategies that can be used to reduce costs and gain more profits.

4) Reducing your shipping time

Usually, amazon sellers can opt for an option called FBM while creating a seller account. FBM is defined as Fulfilled by the merchant. That is amazon lists the product on its website and when someone purchases it the merchant should ship it all by himself or the third-party courier services he links up with. Sellers from eBay, which is another famous e-commerce selling platform use this way of sending the orders usually and is often ridiculed for its late shipping.

For this exact reason, Amazon has smartly linked up with courier services all around the world with hundreds of equipped warehouses to form the most reliable logistic systems. When you get registered with Amazon FBA, Amazon fulfils every order that is processed. However, it charges a basic percentage of the price for the maintenance and many factors come along in between while shipping the products to the customers.

Many Amazon FBA sellers at the beginning suffer to understand the mechanism of the shipping and delay the process of shipping the products to the warehouses with good packaging. This book will give a detailed systematic instruction to decrease the shipping time and costs with different strategies and principles.

5) Marketing

The most important thing amazon sellers should take care of is to get people through the listing page. Successful sellers use various strategies to market the product page. The most reliable strategy is to give PPA ads through social networking platforms like Facebook and Twitter. However, nowadays there has been a lot of competition for the ad space and made sellers improve their marketing tactics. Many Amazon FBA sellers rely on both Amazon ads and amazon associates who promote products for them. In this book, we will give a complete checklist of marketing techniques that can be followed to increase the conversion rate of the product.

6) Getting rid of the product hijackers

When your product goes viral, it is often bound to get hijacked by other sellers by counterfeiting those using irrelevant and illegal tactics. Amazon FBA sellers should be smart enough to detect these counterfeiters and report them to Amazon as soon as possible. To make these product hijackers do not affect your sales in the future you should try to create brand awareness about your product. This book in the further chapters will help you with strategies that can reduce the probability of your products being hijacked. We will also look at different legal procedures that need to take care of at the end of this book.

Advantages of Amazon FBA business

a) Amazon prime

Amazon offers a special subscription program called amazon prime that delivers products at high speed and offer high discount prices. Only amazon FBA sellers are eligible for delivering their products for prime customers thus making the Amazon FBA program a must for people who are targeting prime customers. Prime customers are usually the most top buyers who are likely to buy products from amazon. If you opt-out Amazon FBM program you will lose a whole set of users of the Amazon e-commerce platform.

b) Competitive pricing

Whenever a product is, displayed prime customers get free shipping delivery. This makes the overall price less than the merchant fulfilled program and results in more sales. Competitive pricing attracts a lot more sales for Amazon FBA sellers.

c) Trusted customer service

Amazon FBA sellers get the customer care support of amazon platform for their orders processed. If you are not an Amazon FBA seller you need to partner with third party call Centre services to get good customer care service. With Amazon FBA business, you will get one of the most affordable customer care services with very minimal charges.

d) Return service

Returning the products is one of the difficult things to do if you are shipping the products by yourself. However, with

Amazon FBA the whole process becomes smoother as the amazon delivery partners will also take care of product returns and replacements.

e) Distribution of orders from other channels

Amazon logistics can use your inventory stored in Amazon Operations Centre to distribute orders from other sales channels. You will manage inventory through a simple online user interface and can instruct us to return the inventory at any time.

f) Gift packaging and timer function

Amazon FBA sellers also offer special services like gift-wrapping for very minimal costs. Amazon prime buyers also get a timer function that tracks every shipment and calculate an estimated time for the delivery.

As we have a good peak on the advantages of the FBA business in the next section, we will look at some of the disadvantages that the Amazon FBA business model comes up with. It is important to know about the drawbacks too for scaling up and working hard.

Disadvantages involving in Amazon FBA business

a) Higher costs

It is obvious by now that Amazon FBA consists of excellent logistics systems but comes with higher costs than domestic courier systems. Amazon costs also depend upon the weight of the packages. Therefore, if you are selling cheap products with high shipping weight then you are going to earn very fewer profits as an Amazon FBA seller.

b) High warehousing requirements

Even though FBA sellers are bound to send all their packages to amazon warehouses, all those initial packages should be store in their warehouses. This results in looking for huge workspaces and costs you a ton of money if you are a seller from urban areas.

c) Poor flexibility

As a seller, you will have very little information about the packages that you have seen until it is updated on your tracking shipment page. Amazon offers very bad flexibility between warehouse workers and sellers. Therefore, you need to make sure that everything is okay before sending your shipments to one of your warehouses.

d) Inconvenient return and replacement if they are of foreign suppliers

A lot of FBA sellers depend on suppliers from China to manufacture their products. If there is any return or replacement request by the consumer then it takes at least two weeks, as shipments need to arrive from international warehouses. This may irk some buyers and can result in negative reviews.

With this, we have given a good overview of the disadvantages of the Amazon FBA seller program. The next we will talk about the mindset that needs to be developed by amateur Amazon FBA sellers to achieve good results.

The mindset to be developed for better profits using Amazon FBA

a) Not a get quick rich scheme

Remember that Amazon selling model is not a get quick rich scheme. You need to work hard and constantly monitor your results for months consistently to get good profits. You need to be smart enough to discontinue the listing if you are facing losses. Many people think that the Amazon selling model does not need any research and inventory preparation. However, you need to understand that Amazon can make you a good income source if you do serious physical and mental hard work for it.

b) Hardworking

Imagine waking up early in the morning packing the shipments for your next day deliveries? Isn't it tough? Nevertheless, that is what you are going to do in your initial days. You need to pack your inventory with Amazon's designated labelled shipping. You may get irked with all the procedures that Amazon follows for their delivery partners to take the shipments. Always have a hardworking enthusiasm for your business. Soon you can use your profits to outsource workers to work for your packing procedures. Nevertheless, in the initial stages, you need to learn by your own experience.

c) Workspace for storing products

A good workspace is essential for storing all your product shipments and inventory. It would be difficult to order and ship them in your home. It is always essential to rent a garage near to your home as a workspace. As your business, increases you need to have the mindset of expanding your workspaces too.

d) Investing time for research and looking out

Successful sellers are the ones who do understand market trends with a lot of research and find viral products. You need to develop a mindset of constantly following several newsletters, blogs, and podcasts to understand the new trends and techniques being used by the Amazon sellers. You also need to have guts to outsource products from different retailers and manufacturers. Huge profits come only with huge risks.

e) Passion for marketing and sales

Amazon business is 50% about outsourcing and the other 50% is about driving sales through marketing. You need to be always updated with the latest marketing strategies and tactics that can be used for increasing sales. Understand the importance of the Amazon associate program and approach affiliate marketers for promoting your products on their websites. In the next chapters of this book, we will discuss various marketing strategies like advertising and social media marketing in detail. Have a passion for making out sales and increasing your positive reviews on the Amazon platform.

f) Dream to grow big and expand the business

A good businessman believes in expanding his business. Always dream big and start investing in other niches. Hire workers to make your work easy with the shipment procedures and start expanding the workspaces and your products. Always monitor the sales and recruit an accountant to look at your tax information. Dream big and never get satisfied with small profits.

That's it, with this we have completed a thorough introduction to the Amazon FBA business. In the next chapter, we will start with creating an Amazon FBA account and proceed further with the beginner level products that can be used to sell on the Amazon website. Let us go!

Chapter 2: Basic overview of FBA and signing up

In this chapter, we will start with a section that describes the prerequisites that need to be done before starting an Amazon FBA business. We will next move on to the section where we create an Amazon FBA professional account and learn how to create listings. This chapter mainly focuses on making the user comfortable with the environment he needs to work with. Let us start!

Prerequisites for Amazon FBA

Amazon sellers who are experimenting new with the FBA platform should be well aware that you need to be equipped with an inventory that can be used for packing the products with amazon labels to be sent to the nearest Amazon warehouse.

Here are some of the materials you need to be ready with for better productivity:

a) A decent computer

You need a good working computer for handling all the orders and maintaining track of the data. Get equipped yourself with a good internet connection for fast updates from the amazon system. If you are too busy with shipping the products to a warehouse, you can even hire an amazon virtual assistant that could do simple tasks like finding profitable products and doing research about them.

Always try to use dual monitors for better productivity. Divide the shipping tracking among one monitor and leave the other one for negotiating with suppliers.

b) Laser printer

Amazon has a strict rule of using laser printers for creating labels. Labels are important to easily distinguish and order them according to their shipping location. Therefore, it is a good idea to invest money in a good laser printer for faster shipping.

c) A good smartphone

Nowadays you can track all the order processing data using smartphones effectively. If you are not in the inventory, you can quickly track the information using amazon developed smartphone apps in both Android and iOS. So, invest yourself in a good smartphone for faster access to the analytical data.

d) Wagner heat gun and Scooty peelers

When you get products from your suppliers you need to quality check them first and pack them according to amazon packing procedures. You can use a Wagner heat gun that can quickly remove the labels. Heat gun applies a little bit of heat on the label and makes it come loose. If you combine a heat gun with scooty peelers, you can remove the labels very quickly and can check the products that have been shipped by the manufacturers.

e) Dymo thermal labels

While shipping you need to paste the standard Amazon FBA item label that is Dymo thermal labels on the packages. Remember that you need to use these labels a lot so buy them a lot at once for saving some money.

f) Bubble wraps

If you are packaging sensitive products or products with glass, it is important to enclose them in bubble wraps for the customers. Amazon has made bubble wraps mandatory for certain items for minimizing future mishaps. So, get your inventory filled with bubble wraps and bubble sheets to enclose the products.

g) Shipping scale

Whenever you are shipping your packages, it is important to weight the package size as shipping costs may differ with the weight of the packages. You can find shipping rates for different weighing scales on the amazon website. For this reason, you need to invest yourself with a good shipping scale that gives accurate values.

h) Wireless barcode scanner

Barcodes are used for easy tracking of the packages. When the barcode is scanned both the customer and seller will get real-time information on their tracking shipment pages. Amazon provides barcodes on the seller central page for all the listings that have been ordered. All you need to do is laser print and scan them before sending to the Amazon warehouse. For this reason, it is important to buy a good wireless barcode scanner.

i) A good camera

Whenever there is a new listing, it is important to post images to increase your conversion rates. You can use images that are taken with smartphones at initial stages, but it will be good you can invest in a good photographic camera to increase sales.

With this, we have completed basic prerequisites that are essential for an Amazon FBA business. In the next section, we will look at the sign-up process in detail. Let us go!

Create an amazon FBA account

Amazon offers many services on the platform and it is not necessary to create a new account for every service they are offering. For the Amazon seller account, you just need to log in with your amazon buyer account email and password. Make sure that you have activated two-factor authentication for better safety.

a) After logging into the Amazon account at the top toolbar find the menu that displays sell. Click it and you will be taken to a page that displays the Amazon FBA program. For some users, a 30-day trial is offered but remember that it is user-specific, and some country users may not get a trial account.

b) You will have an option to select the type of Amazon FBA account. Amazon offers two types of seller accounts named as individual and professional. If you are short in capital investment, you can experiment at first with the individual account that charges no monthly fees. However, remember that an individual account can only handle 40 orders per month and if you exceed that amount, you need to switch to a professional account. Amazon's individual account is perfect for sellers with very fewer orders.

c) The second type of account is amazon FBA professional account, which is famous among sellers all over the world. Statistics say that more than 70% of Amazon FBA sellers use a professional account for better delivery of products. Amazon FBA professional, unlike individual accounts, charges 40$ per month, (this excludes Amazon FBA charges for every order that is placed). Amazon's professional seller account also gets access to amazon analytical tools that can be used to increase the sales of the product.

d) After selecting the desired seller account type, you need to enter the tax information of the seller. This gets us to a discussion about the legal business name that you need to fill in the sign-up form.

Usually, Amazon FBA sellers fall under two categories that are namely sole-proprietorship and Private LLC. We will discuss these two entities in detail.

a) sole-proprietorship

This is the easiest way to get into the Amazon FBA business. Even though it has some cons that are not preferable when your business expands but it is still the best option for single investors trying to start their Amazon journey. We will list both the pros and cons below in detail for your better understanding.

Pros of the sole proprietorship

a) First of all, it is very easy to get started with Amazon FBA because all you need is your tax number and social security number. There is no need to get any other clearances.

b) There is no need to submit or list any other documents for the acceptance of the FBA program.

Cons of the sole proprietorship

a) You are liable for every transaction that happens. You are responsible for every loan that has been taken and you should make sure that you would pay those mortgages on time. If not, the Loan money will be recovered from your assets.

b) When your business starts expanding you will get a lot of bills and tax cuts that will confuse other businesses tax information that you are dealing with.

c) The major disadvantage of a sole proprietorship is some of the manufactures will be willing to work only with trusted organizations to avoid wastage of their time. If you are wishing to import your products from Chinese manufacturers this will be a major disadvantage.

For this reason, we suggest you get aware of other tax categories that are private LLC (Limited liability Company). This means that you register your amazon FBA business on a business name with a FEIN number. Federal departments suggest you proceed with this for different tax liabilities and security reasons. We will discuss both the pros and cons of Private LLC in detail here.

Pros of private LLC

a) You are not liable for every loan that has been taken on the business name. That is, banks have no right to liquidate or dissolve your assets for clearing their loans.

b) In a sole proprietorship, while taxing you may pay extra taxation called double taxation because you are Ineligible for tax returns. However, with private LLC you will get tax returns on your tax.

c) Chinese manufacturers will be more interested to work with a trusted company with FEIN and can deliver a huge quantity of goods. This recognition as a limited liability company will be a trustworthy sign for manufacturers.

Cons of the private LLC

a) It takes a lot of time to get started with a limited liability company. You need to be registered with many government entities and need to pay a mandatory amount to get the process are completed.

b) You need to understand many tax-related terms and should maintain accountings perfectly. For this, you need to recruit a chartered accountant, which costs a hefty amount.

c) Banks will not give direct loans to the limited liability companies as they are surrounded by many complications. Your loan hunting process will become a lot more difficult if you opt for this option.

d) After entering the tax information such as social security number and FEIN Amazon will ask you to go through a simple tax tour. Make sure that you enter all the required information without any mistakes.

e) In the next step, you need to select the Store name. Make sure you select a good name that is not generic and confusing. Brainstorm many ideas and confirm with a catchy store name that can be easily inserted into the buyer's minds. You cannot change your store name in the future so make sure you are completely satisfied with the name.

f) At the end of the form enter your phone number so that Amazon will verify your identity with a pin. Enter the pin and your account is live on the Amazon FBA.

g) After entering the homepage of your seller account, you will be prompted to select the products that you are wishing to sell. It is better to select every item that is available in the options. However, remember that amazon restricts some of the products for selling. To sell the products in this category you need to send the listing to Amazon for verification and if Amazon approves then you are good to go with that product.

With this, we have completed a brief introduction about the sign-up process of the amazon FBA seller account. In the next section, we will get accustomed to some of the elements in the seller central. Let us go!

Costs in FBA

This section will give a brief explanation about the expenses for which FBA charges. Understanding these prices will help you understand the mechanism of the FBA seller program and both the pros and cons of this business model.

Amazon FBA cost is typically divided into five sections as below:

a) Order distribution fee

This fee is allied for the delivery of the products using an amazon efficient logistics system. This order distribution depends on the size and weight of the shipment.

b) FBA inventory storage fee

This fee is applied when a shipment needs to stay in an Amazon warehouse. For a significant time, the fees will be less but if the product stays in the inventory for more than a month than the inventory, storage will start rising according to amazon regulations.

c) Order removal fee

If an order is removed by the user, a small fee will be applied by the amazon on its sellers for the resources that have been used.

d) Return processing fee

If the customer has raised a return ticket of the product the FBA seller needs to pay the return processing fee as the amazon logistics system will return the product to your inventory without any damages.

e) Unplanned processing service fee

Sometimes shipments may reach unplanned processing checkpoints due to various customs regulations. For some of these varied reasons, amazon makes an unplanned processing service fee for this.

Creating a listing in amazon seller central

If you are all aware of the fees of the amazon FBA, then it is the time to start your listing from the amazon central. Follow the below instructions to create your listing.

1) Go to your Amazon seller dashboard and enter the inventory section.

2) When you are in the inventory section you will find an option that says add a new product. Click on it and you are ready to start your listing.

3) First of all, enter the name of the listing and continue with the listing creation process where you will upload images, write descriptions and specifications. Amazon also allows you to add product videos. You also need to add categories and keywords for your listing.

4) At the last step select the price that you wish your product wants to be and submit the listing. Within a few minutes, your product page will go live on the Amazon website.

With this, we have completed a brief introduction to the Amazon FBA program and in the next chapter; we will discuss the Amazon A9 algorithm that is responsible for displaying search results for amazon in detail. Let us go!

Chapter 3: Mastering Amazon Algorithm techniques

Start Amazon is a crowded marketplace where thousands of retailers and sellers try to climb up to the top search result for a product listing. Just like Google, which uses different search, engine-ranking techniques to rank its SERP Amazon also uses an algorithm known as the A9 algorithm that determines the top results for a keyword or product category? In this chapter, we will explain in detail the techniques that sellers should be aware of to increase their ranking for the product they are willing to sell. Let us go!

What is the A9 algorithm and how is it different from Google algorithms?

Google has been a pioneer in search engine technology for a decade and the most important reason for the success of Google is its complex algorithms that display valid results according to the user's search query using various criteria like backlinks and less duplicate content. However, Amazon works on a different model where it tries to sell the consumers a product unlike in Google where consumers are the product (by selling ads, or by making users use their other services like YouTube).

This difference has made Amazon develop an efficient algorithm called A9 algorithm that tracks every move that the user takes while he was using amazon and its affiliated websites. For this reason, it was now believed that Amazon has access to a huge chunk of information that no one ever possesses in its cloud. Amazon integrates this data with it is hardcore data mining and data analysis algorithms that can query the search results according to the user's wishes and tastes. This sum up to the conclusion that Google's algorithms give us results that are the most accurate for search query whereas Amazon algorithms give results that are more relevant to the user tastes and past behaviour.

Amazon FBA sellers who are trying to sell products should consider this and try to improve the rank of the product using the following techniques that are believed to be used by the A9 algorithm to determine results. The next section will look at this in detail.

Amazon algorithm focuses on mainly three goals to determine what to show for its customers. These are the only criteria that amazon cares about and will always. Sometimes Amazon may be harsh on sellers because at the end of the day, all it cares about is satisfying customers and that is the reason why it has been ruling the e-commerce industry from the past few years.

Here are the major goals that amazon want to accomplish with its algorithm:

a) To make customers come back often

Amazon sells many products from safety pins to motorcycles. The only way it can sustain in this competitive industry is by not losing a customer for any reason. To make this happen Amazon introduced a new service called amazon prime that would deliver the products without any shipping charges. Amazon has taken a huge risk with this because of the huge number of orders it needs to be delivered within a short frame of time.

Thanks to Amazon's efficient logistics system, it has grabbed a large portion of market share and is now thriving with profits. Amazon offers various offers and discounts to make customers come back to shop with the e-commerce platform. Amazon A9 algorithm makes sure that products are displayed in a way that the customers would spend more on the platform.

b) To understand the conversion factors

Amazon tracks many factors like bouncing rate, quality of images to determine what are the essentials that are making users buy the products. This self-analysis of product pages can make amazon improve its quarterly sales.

c) Improve its product relevancy search

Amazon has many consumers who are trying to buy a product without a complete understanding of the product they are going to buy. Therefore, amazon uses its efficient algorithms to data mine all the descriptions, product titles, and images to give a perfect result for the customer. By using the A9 algorithm amazon gets this awesome curating feature that can help both the e-commerce company sellers and the end-users.

Amazon never disclosed the factors they consider for the implementation of the A9 algorithm, but many third-party sources have identified the metrics that Amazon uses to rank the products that are available in their platform. In this section, we will discuss some of these metrics in detail. Follow along for a better understanding of the topic.

1) Negative seller feedback

Whenever a customer buys a product on amazon, he is eligible to send feedback about the product and the seller. Feedback can be given either by text, email or by the amazon feedback window that is present beside the order details. It is believed that amazon tracks this feedback information to improve its search algorithm. Any wrong feedback related to the products will be filtered and will become judgmental for displaying the results. Therefore, for this reason, all the Amazon FBA sellers should prefer quality as their major weapon. Always try to give customers a perfect product so that there will be very little negative feedback and thus good Amazon search ranking.

2) Order processing speed

This is the reason why FBM sellers are not present in the top search pages usually. Amazon logistic systems are told to be given faster processing time and can deliver the products within a week at a maximum. However, Amazon FBA sellers should be sending their products to warehouses and huge order numbers may delay the order processing speed. So, always make sure that you have enough quantity in the warehouses.

3) In stock rate

Sometimes when you visit a product page, you will be welcomed with an "out of stock "message. This briefly details that, now, the product is not available in the Amazon warehouse, and cannot be ordered until the seller gives an intimation about the stock details. You may lose many sales due to this message and for this reason, amazon prefers sellers with stock in their warehouses. So, always make sure that you can deliver goods if there is an increase in demand for your products.

A quick search of products can make you understand more about this metric. Go to the Amazon website, enter any product of your wish, and scroll on to the results that are displayed. Look at the individual product pages and you will find that almost all products have enough stock. Thus, it should be remembered that the in-stock rate is directly proportional to your amazon search rank.

4) perfect order percentage

When a customer orders the product, it goes on various stages until it is delivered to the buyer. It will go through the technical listing, shipping, and delivery. If a customer is satisfied with all the stages about the order than the perfect order percentage of the seller increases. Amazon estimates the perfect order percentage using different data mining algorithms and uses those results to display search results. So, if you are consistent in every department during the order processing your POP increases and naturally your sales too.

5) Order defect rate

Amazon customers are hard to deal with. If there is any problem with the product that has been shipped to the consumer, they can complain about it to amazon buyer protection. So always, make sure that your product is of good quality and try to send it to amazon warehouse within less time frame. Every bad feedback can increase your order defect rate, which is said to be preferred by the A9 algorithm to filter results. However, when you are shipping with Amazon FBA, all shipping delays will be responsible by amazon and the algorithm that orders defect rate will not affect you. Also, never, try to claim to provide a buyback guarantee if you are not willing to offer it to your customers. Consumers may report to amazon for giving fake claims, which will increase your order defect rate.

6) Exit rate

When your listing is live, users will visit the amazon product page from various sources or directly from the amazon search engine. It is believed that an average amazon customer only stays for a few seconds on a product page. When a customer leaves without ordering or prime ordering any product this statistic entity is defined as the exit rate according to amazon standards. If the exit rate is more than 75%, of all the visits the product page has received then the listing may receive some demerits in the Amazon A9 algorithm. So, always make sure every detail of the listing is provided along with beautiful images and description such that the visitor will get tempted to place the order. A decrease in exit rate is good for both sales and page rank for a keyword.

7) Packing options

When the product gets delivered customers are concerned about the type of package that has been done to the product. If there is any unsealed protection for sensitive products, there are huge chances for customers giving negative feedback. This is the major reason why amazon FBM sellers get negative ratings. However, if you are an Amazon FBA seller amazon looks after the safe sealed packaging in their warehouses thus reducing the negative reviews and improving your search index in the results.

8) Sales rank

Whenever you visit amazon you might have seen sales rank in the category section. This is the metric that attracts many visitors and can help you gather more sales. Good keyword research and initial marketing strategies can help to increase your product rank in that category. A lot of people give away their products at initial stages to improve their sales rank as it has a tremendous impact on conversion. It is highly believed that amazon values sales rank and can help you sit at the top of the results page.

You may wonder whether it is easy to surpass the competitors and increase your sales rank. Research says that it is possible to improve your sales rank with good competitor research and initial sales.

9) Customer reviews

Amazon A9 algorithm also highly depends on customer reviews to filter the results. You can give quick research on any product category and can observe that the results are of high customer ratings. This is the reason why many Amazon FBA sellers use fake review agencies to get positive reviews. However, never try to cheat the system as it may lead to negative consequences. Always deliver the consumers a satisfactory product so that they will give positive reviews as a token of appreciation. Amazon also considers quality than quantity. This essential algorithmic trick has made Amazon a bad place for junk and cheap products.

10) Answered questions

Whenever you visit an amazon product page you might have saw a section that consists of questions and answers from the consumers and the seller. This is a very essential conversion factor and can increase sales. An additional advantage of questions & answers in amazon is even buyers can share their knowledge about the product. Due to this whenever a visitor is interested to buy a product, he can clear his doubts about the product and conversion rate increases. So, always try to update your listing with a lot of questions and answers, as the Amazon A9 algorithm prefers it highly.

11) Quality of images

Images are the most driving factor for sales. Recently Amazon has a rule that makes 1000 x 1000 pixels images mandatory for every listing. If you are unable to provide high-quality images A9 algorithm adds your listing into suppressed listings.

With 1000 x 1000 pixels, you can get a hover zoom option and can look at the product closely. Close sources from Amazon say that in the coming year's amazon will introduce 3D renders that can improve the visual experience of amazon customers. To rank well in Amazon search results, you need to invest in a good photographic camera for making believable images that can intrigue the visitors.

12) Prices

Pricing is a controversial topic and is often difficult to say whether amazon uses it for ranking its results or not. Many experiments by the search engine optimization specialists confirmed that amazon indeed uses price as a ranking factor for few categories. However, still, positive reviews are the most driving factor. Therefore, if you are getting good positive reviews for your listing then you may try to reduce the prices for few days to increase your organic search and sales.

13) parent-child products

Usually, Amazon FBA sellers sell multiple products of the same listing with different colours and sizes. Imagine if you are selling apparel with an American flag on it. You have it in different colours and product types such as shirts, tank tees, and hoodies. Amazon offers you a solution to display all of them on one product page instead of different product pages. This grouping of parent-child products can help in the increase in visitors and sales. For this reason, it is believed that the amazon A9 algorithm prefers parent-child products over single products.

14) Time on page and bounce rate

Amazon determines the quality of the listing using two different metrics that are often unnoticed. We will describe these two metrics in detail in this section.

a) Staying time on the product page

This is a metric that is often used by amazon to determine the quality of the listing. Amazon collects the time spent by a visitor on a particular page and compares it with the other product pages to determine the search engine results. It is also a high conversion factor when compared to other metrics. If a listing has intrigued and made the seller, stay for a long time then the amazon algorithm weighs it higher than the other product pages. It is logical because a bad product can never intrigue the buyers.

b) Bounce rate

There is a small difference between bounce rate and time on a page that often goes unnoticed due to various factors. Bounce rate is defined as a numerical entity in seconds, which defines the user switching depending on the product offers or sponsored items. The bounce rate is inversely proportional to the impact on the A9 algorithm. If the bounce rate is more on your product page, then you are lucky enough to find your spot on the top results page. Amazon FBA sellers should prepare intriguing product pages with brand images to make visitors hooked about your listing.

15) Product listing completeness

This metric sums up all the conversion factors we have discussed in the previous sections. Amazon A9 algorithm prefers a product page that consists of all the restrictions that amazon has imposed on sellers. If there is the completeness of the product page, then the amazon algorithm may demerit you from their results. Therefore, it is always important to maintain your product page with complete information. From the next metric, we discuss all metrics which fall under the relevancy factor that amazon considers for its A9 algorithm.

16) Product title

The title is the most important metric that the A9 algorithm considers while grouping out similar rests. This is the reason why you need to concentrate on researching a little bit more on keyword research for the product title. Amazon allows you to enter 80 characters for the product title so brainstorm the best keyword ideas so that you will get good organic search. However, do not stuff unnecessary and meaningless words for the sake of ranking is it may be useless for the listing relevancy.

17) Product features

The second metric where keywords are highly considered is on the product features section. Product features are also known as the bullet points in the product overview category. These are the glance section that visitors look at most of the times. Try to insert many long-tail keywords in the product features for better recognition of the amazon A9 algorithm.

18) Product description

Amazon product page conveys a lot of information in the form of a descriptive paragraph. A lot of sellers write very fewer descriptions to their products thinking that it may not be an indicator for amazon SERP. However, experiments have shown that descriptions that are filled with a long tail and short tail keywords are likely to outperform other listings. Write a simple non-technical description so that the visitors can understand the essence and usage of your product. You can also use some Catchy phrases to obtain their attention.

19) Brand and manufacturer part

Amazon highly considers branded products as their top search results. Amazon algorithms check whether your product has been registered on the amazon brand registry and pushes you forward if are registered. The manufacturer is also displayed on the left side of the product page. This is the reason why you need to ask your Alibaba suppliers if they already have clients selling on Amazon. Manufacturers with past selling records in Amazon are favoured over the newcomers.

20) Specifications

Product specifications are an easy way to give a complete overview of your product with numerical entities. Many products available in amazon are not thorough with specifications. Specifications come into handy when visitors want to filter the results using colour, size, prices, and weight. Amazon offers many filters using the advanced search. So thorough specifications of your product can bring some new visitors with a thorough understanding of what they need to buy. Amazon A9 algorithm favours products with very well written specifications.

21) Category and sub-category

Amazon divides its infinite products with well-distinguished categories. If you want to look at all the Amazon categories, you can visit the amazon home page and can click on the category's toolbar. This is an easy way for Amazon users to find their desired products. A lot of reports said that amazon users prefer using the category menu for finding their products rather than by an Amazon search engine. Some examples of categories are Furniture, health, pets, and Apparel.

Categories are further divided into subcategories and are introduced to choose the products easily. Some of the examples of subcategories include pet supplies, office furniture, and Men footwear. Apart from serving as easy navigation to users' categories and subcategories are also used as a metric for a search engine algorithm.

Whenever a seller creates a listing, he is opted to select categories for displaying his listing in those product results. Choosing categories and subcategories is important because of this factor. Amazon A9 algorithm uses this factor as a high majority filtering technique for all the available products.

22) Search terms

Apart from selecting product categories, amazon sellers are also made to select 50 search terms for their listing. A lot of users usually enter the 10 search terms, but it is useful if you can enter the 50 search terms. If you are not comfortable with this, you can use an amazon search term generator to do this work for you. Amazon A9 algorithm gives a high weight to search terms when it is filtering the results for the consumer.

23) Source keyword

This is one of the most hidden pathways to cracking the amazon A9 algorithm. Whenever you enter a product page, a URL address is generated. You can manually change the URL of your listing in the seller central.

For example, here is an URL:

www.amazon.com/furniture?hejd=!377/keywords=office+chair

Here you might have observed that the end part of the URL is favoured by the Amazon A9 algorithm and if someone visits the URL, the algorithm thinks that this is a good result for the following keyword. A lot of users use this cloaking method to rank quickly in Amazon results. However, remember that it is not always reliable, and Amazon may soon change its URL cloaking system. However, below we explain the strategy to easily rank in the Amazon SERP page 1.

Strategy using URL shorteners.

a) Register yourself with a premium URL shortening service. Do not register with free URL shorteners as they may sell your data to third party services.

b) Using the shortening service make the URL short and share it with amazon associate partners to let them use it in their websites and whenever someone clicks that URL you are tricking amazon that the visitor has come to the product page using the source keywords. This strategy helps you to rank for the keywords in very less time.

24) Amazon enhanced brand content

Amazon offers a program that clearly distinguishes normal products from branded products. You will have a trusted badge that mentions your logo and brand name. Make sure that you use the same logo in all your products. Registering in amazon enhanced brand content program can help you rank better in Amazon for being a trustworthy seller.

With this, we have completed a detailed discussion about the Amazon A9 algorithm and the responsible factors. We have given clear examples with layman explanations for many factors. In the next chapter, we will start learning about some of the negotiation techniques that need to be used to attract foreign suppliers to manufacture products for you. Let us go!

Chapter 4: Negotiation with Alibaba suppliers

This chapter is very essential for newbies in the business because negotiation is the basic principle of minimizing unnecessary costs. A lot of retail suppliers and manufacturers are willing to work with their clients if the seller is serious about his business. Every manufacturer wishes for a long-term relationship with their clients and it is your responsibility to make the manufacturers feel that you are serious about what you are doing. This chapter will give you various strategies that can be used to negotiate perfectly with suppliers. Let us go!

Where can we find suppliers?

Outsourcing products is one of the most important skills and can be done by various methods. We will discuss some of these outsourcing methods in our upcoming chapters. If you are starting on Amazon FBA business, it is suggested to order form Chinese suppliers from Alibaba for higher profits. A lot of people get a false impression on Chinese products due to different reasons such as bad quality, duplicate products and are often afraid because of the trade wars that go between the USA and China. However, as of now, it is very profitable to sell products that are imported from Chinese suppliers after a check on the quality of the products by yourself.

In this section, we will give a systematic instruction to negotiate with manufacturers in Alibaba for your product outsourcing. Follow along to learn the basics of Seller negotiation tactics.

Step by step instruction to negotiate with Alibaba suppliers:

1) First of all, do complete research on the product that you are going to sell as your listing. Complete research consists of analysing the competitor prices and specifications of the products they are selling. When you are satisfied with the information obtained, insert them in a PowerPoint presentation or Infographics for easy presentation to the sellers.

2) Remember that you are communicating with people who are not proficient in English. So, always use simple English words in your emails to make them understand better. Also, remember that you both are in different time zones and do not expect a message until midnight. Respect their work timings.

3) First of all, login to Alibaba website using your credentials and search the category or product you are looking to selling on Amazon. Alibaba filters and gives you the most relevant

wholesale suppliers and industry people looking for clients. You can manually check them for a better understanding of the Chinese retail environment.

4) In the next step create a post with your product requirements and specifications in detail. Mention that you are looking forward to a long relationship and ask them to quote their prices for the offer. You can use English, or you can hire a translator to input the information for you.

5) After posting on the Alibaba site you will get offers from various sellers in high volume. However closely monitor and reply to sellers that have an Alibaba trusted badge in their account. This is a trustworthy symbol given by the Alibaba website after successful verification.

6) Now after looking at the quotes by the sellers and your requirements select the top 10 sellers from the list and individually email them with a format that we give below. Do not forget to use simple words in all the emails.

Email negotiation Template

a) Mention your business and give your FEIN address if you have any in the initial paragraph. This helps the Chinese supplier understand that they are dealing with a serious seller looking for a product.

b) Frame questions in a way such that they are required to answer. If you do not get a response from the supplier, do not try to do business with them. As per current trends, only 60% of the suppliers reply to emails to their clients. So, make sure you find your best supplier who can communicate with you. If you find an enthusiasm to work with your products from their replies, consider them as your suppliers.

c) Check the profile statistics of the manufacturer on the Alibaba website. You can ask some of them even their website for further verification. Alibaba tracks all the orders that have been placed using Alibaba and gives you buyer protection. It is better not to contact them using third-party services like WhatsApp and we chat for business negotiations.

d) Ask their prices and push them to accept your required price. Email them the screenshots of other quotes that offer fewer prices. Nevertheless, do not try to push your prices too low far away from reality. At the end of the day, understand quality is the most important thing for your business.

e) Ask them about their manufacturing procedures and quality guidelines. The best way to verify the quality is by asking sample pieces for money. You can even book a slot of Chinese mediators to check the quality of the products for you. You can find these quality checkers from some of the Chinese websites. Make sure you use these strategies to minimize the time of your first delivery.

After sending an email template to your suppliers, you will receive replies from some of the enthusiastic suppliers who are willing to work with you. Verify again from the Alibaba website and give a nod to work with them. Make sure you give good prototypes and specifications of your product for them to start manufacturing the product. In the next section, we will discuss a procedure that can help you express the desired product qualities that you are expecting from your suppliers.

Making suppliers understand the Product, you are expecting

a) First of all, do thorough research on the product you are trying to sell. Check the competitors in the category, analyse their prices, and estimate their profits. Use third-party tools to monitor their estimated sales and list out the specification and features.

b) Order your competitor products and analyse them in person. Understand the build quality of the product and make prototypes using a good designer. If you are good on a budget, you can even create a 3D render protocol for better communication.

c) List out all the changes that you are expecting from your competitor products.

Remember that an exact replication of the competitor's product is called counterfeiting and may land you in trouble. Always try to change the build quality and add some more features to the product for making your product unique and usable than others.

Here is an example template:

Hi supplier,

I want a private labelled product like this juice maker. This juice maker consists of aluminium foils for cutting the fruits. I want it to be built of more high quality and I need you to add a vegetable mixer at the bottom of the juice mixer. This serves as a dual-purpose juice mixer for both vegetables and fruits. I want these to be manufactured in three colours black, red and blue respectively. I have attached the 3D render and brand images for your understanding. Please ask without hesitation if you have any further queries.

Thank you,

Sam private LLC.

Additional things to be negotiated with the suppliers:

a) Handling deposits

Deposits are a crucial matter of negotiation for both suppliers and sellers. If you are willing to give a high discount there, are high chances for suppliers sending the shipments soon? However, this is not an ideal world and you should not deposit many amounts initially when it is your first shipment from the manufacturer.

You need to first verify the quality of the products using an overseas quality checker and then proceed with the deposit negotiations. Whenever you are asked to give a 60% deposit before the shipment you need to negotiate about lowering the prices and increasing the quality of the products.

Deposits are transferred to Chinese suppliers usually by PayPal and western union. It is easier for sellers from the United States to send money via PayPal as it is simpler forward, but a lot of Chinese suppliers are not satisfied with PayPal as they charge large amounts as commissions. For this reason, you need to be equipped with western union services to do wire transfers.

b) Negotiation of prices

The pricing for shipments usually depends on the number of units you are trying to make a deal with the manufacturer. In layman terms, the number of units of the product is inversely proportional to the price. Therefore, if you are ordering very fewer units then you may have less success while dealing with the price negotiation. If you are unable to get a price reduction from the manufacturers, then ask them to increase quality and ask them fast shipping procedures to seal the deal.

c) The decrease in prices for high volume

As said before many Alibaba suppliers will work only for high quantity supplies, as they will not cater to profits if done in less volume. If you are starting with a small capital start with small products that can be ordered in high quantities. If you are ordering, a high number of products ask for price negotiation with an agreement of paying the deposits at the initial stages. This can help you reduce some costs in manufacturing the products.

d) Requesting samples

Many Amazon FBA sellers are not sure about the quality of the products even if they are private-labelled products. It is a good practice to ask the manufacturer for sample pieces for the first shipment of course with a favourable price for both you and the manufacturer. When the products come from the international warehouses via ship or by air check them immediately in the ports by yourself. You can hire someone from the product quality section to check the durability and the price value. If you are happy with the sample products, then make a deal with large quantities.

e) Be a good client

As much as sellers expect good products from the manufacturers, they expect the same level of respect from their clients. Always pay the deposit in time and if possible do it by wire transfers, as it is an easy way for them to withdraw the funds. Always send them protocols that are accurate and easy to understand. Understand that sometimes there would be delays due to various reasons. Try to maintain a good relationship with your clients such that they would love to work with you in other products too.

f) Shipping procedures

Shipping is a very complex topic and a messy thing when dealing with international manufacturers and especially China due to the trade wars between the USA and China. Usually, the manufacturers deliver your shipments to the nearest Chinese port with their costs and from there you need to bear the shipping charges for the shipment. If you are good at negotiating, you can request manufacturers for bearing the international shipping charges for the shipments. If you are lucky, some retailers will agree to pay the shipment charges.

g) Letting go of the supplier if they are of low quality or return amount is high

Business is not an easy pathway. As time goes on some of the manufacturers will decrease the quality of the products for various reasons. Use a three-strike policy to determine the quality of the supplier and if they send you, bad quality items even for the third shipment stop doing business with them. Also closely monitor the number of returns that the customers are requesting for your product. This will help you to come to a conclusion about the performance of the product and send them a memo about ending business with them. Do not be too harsh but be polite and act like a professional businessman before leaving out them from your business.

With this, we have learned a lot of negotiation techniques, tricks, and templates that can be used for better business with Chinese Alibaba suppliers. In the next chapter, we will go through keyword research in detail. Keyword research is a complex topic to understand but is very important for driving more sales. Follow along!

Chapter 5: Keyword Research for FBA

This chapter is an introduction to basic and advanced keyword research for Amazon FBA sellers. Keywords are the single entity elements that can help the sellers rank top in the result page. People often get confused between different types of keywords and waste a lot of time implementing wrong strategies to rank on Amazon. As we already discussed in brief in the Amazon A9 algorithm that Keywords hold a prominent position in helping you rank at the top when users search with a long or short-tail keyword. In this chapter, we will, in brief, explain some of the strategies that successful amazon FBA sellers have used from the past few years. We will also give a complete tutorial of keyword tool.io for a better practical understanding of keyword research. Let us go!

What are the keywords?

A keyword is a single entity word or a group of linearly arranged words that have a significant reach for a month in any search engine (either google or amazon) by its users.

Why are keywords important?

First, keywords are an easy way for internet giants to understand what their users are wishing for. Amazon uses all its keyword search metrics to improve its Amazon A9 algorithm and deliver accurate results for the consumers. For seller's analysis of keywords can give a complete understanding of the market trends and where to step into for making profits. Many third-party sellers scrape tons of keywords and metric information to provide accurate estimations for competitor research.

What is the impact of keywords for FBA sellers?

First, remember the fact that both Amazon and its seller's goal is to sell as much as products they can. For this reason, sellers need to carefully analyse the keyword patterns that consumers use to search in Amazon. A lot of consumers that are more than 70% of the Amazon visitors use single-word keywords to search the product they are looking for and the remaining 30% of the users rely on long-tail keywords to search the products. Still confused? Look at the following examples to understand the difference between long-tail and single keywords.

Single keywords:

Bats
Balls
Mobiles
Shirts

Long-tail keywords

Best washing machine
Puma budget level shoes
Good induction stove

This might have given you a good understanding of the difference between both types of keywords. Single keywords have huge competition and it can be very overwhelming and difficult for new sellers to occupy the top results. Due to this fact, many sellers who are new to the platform are suggested to research long-tail keywords and target those users. In the next section, we will give a complete strategy for keyword research using different tools. Follow along!

Here is a five-step guide to doing better keyword research. Apply these principles and you will soon get better results with these keywords.

1) Start with seed keywords

Seed keywords are also known as short-tail keywords that are keywords with only one word. Whenever you start to do keyword research on your product, you need to find a good keyword.

What is a good keyword?

A good keyword is something that can drive you new sales and has a high return on an investment after the advertisement campaigns. Good keywords are often called as gold keywords by the Amazon FBA specialists. Golden keywords often have very little competition and more search volume.

How to find a good seed keyword?

A seed keyword is often used for understanding the scope of your category rather than trying to do PPC ads against them. Even if you do experiment PPC ads with seed keywords you may not have good results because the competition will be extremely high and advertisements in all networks cost a lot higher.

To find a good seed keyword you need to first understand that you need to think like a shopper. If you have found out a product to sell by now, try to think about what a buyer would search for your product to show up. List all those keywords in a paper or an excel sheet and search them in a keyword research tool. Many seed keywords as if for example "bats" have high search volume and competition. This method also helps you to research products for your next sale.

2) Generate keyword ideas

In this section, we will learn some tricks to generate keyword ideas easily. First, write down the niche that you are targeting and mention their demographics. List down the audience that is interested to buy products in your demographics. After listing down brainstorm, the keywords that come to your mind in a piece of paper and try to search them in both google and amazon search engines.

If you enter those root keywords one by one, you will get recommendations for each one of them precisely. Copy all those keywords and place them in an excel sheet for better organization. Now link out those keywords one by one and expand your keyword ideas into a whole another level.

You can further check all these keywords search value and wield out any keywords that have very little search value per month. Use a good keyword research engine like a MOZ explorer to understand your competitors for every keyword. In the next section, we will learn about the importance of keyword metrics and give suggestions to understand them in detail.

3) Analyze keyword metrics

Keyword metrics are the essential factors to decide the importance of the keywords for your product pages and PPC ad campaigns. Here we describe some of the keyword metrics that third-party keyword research tools often use.

Keyword research tools use metrics to let the users understand the importance of a keyword. However, metrics are also considered as an estimation according to the scraping algorithms that the keyword research tools use.

Here are the four most important keyword metrics:

a) The volume of the keyword

This is a metric that all keyword search engines prefer to show up in the first place. Volume here is referred to as the number of times a keyword is searched by the end-users from the Amazon search engine. It is very difficult to target the keywords that have a volume of 1 lakh and above as there will be a lot more competition. Your ideal keyword volume is from 10,000 to 20,000 with less competition. These types of keywords are called golden keywords. Whenever your auto, search keyword metrics use this as a trick to find good keywords. These volume values are often accurate and can help you get a good estimation of popular products and sub-categories.

b) Keyword difficulty

This is a metric that determines the keyword difficulty using various machine-learning algorithms. It is not so ideal to target keywords with high competitors who are paying high prices for each advertisement. Many keyword search engines estimate this data using past ad search criteria and display the difficulty metric besides your keyword. If you are trying to target a keyword that is of 80% keyword difficulty, then it is a complete waste of time and can make you end up in losses. You should try to target keywords with keyword difficulty ranging from 40% - 60% as it is simpler to rank for them within a short time with some good keyword placements in the algorithm driving relevancy factors such as Title, description, and specifications.

c) Click-through rate

The click-through rate is often defined as the number of times the link has been clicked on when it is shown in the top results. Many factors come into force that makes the visitors click on the links and pass through into the product page. Usually, a good click-through rate results in good sales and good interaction with social media posts. Keyword search engines scrape much data to get this click-through rate metric. Always use the highest click-through rate keywords for better results.

d) The priority of the keyword

The priority of the keyword is a special keyword that calculates all the three metrics mentioned above and gives an overall score of the individual keyword. Usually, this score is between 0-10 and anything above 6 is worth trying if.

e) Traffic potential

This keyword metric explains about the number of visits the individual product page has obtained due to the keyword. It is often interesting to find out, which results are preferring, based on the results given. You can sometimes find the nature of your niche audience and can apply them to increase your sales.

With these keyword metrics, you might have got a good understanding of the keyword research and the way to find products that can sell. In the next section, we will learn about grouping these keywords for better advertisement and marketing management.

4) Group your keywords

After noting down all these keywords and keyword metrics in a spreadsheet you need to organize them in a better way for easier access to different advertisement campaigns based on the nature of the ad network you are trying to use them. Here we will list you some tips to group the keywords easily.

a) Divide them according to the number of sales

Sales are the driving factor for increasing your sales velocity and climbing to the top results. Therefore, your priority should always be to focus on the keywords that are driving more sales. After grouping, them according to keyword difficulty from ascending to descending order and focus on the starting part of the list for your business.

b) Divide them according to micro niches

When you look at the top products of your niche, you can easily divide them into micro-niches for easy valuation. While evaluating you will notice the most selling micro-niches in your category. Select this micro-niche and make a separate group of them combining both first and second techniques.

c) Divide them according to search volume

Even though if they are of high difficulty it makes sense to target those keywords who have high search volume and sales. If customers are looking for the products to buy, then it is a classic micro niche for your category. For example, in office furniture, ergonomic chairs are considered a popular keyword and often have
1,000,000 search volume. Group all these keywords and place them in a spreadsheet.

d) Group keywords for PPC advertisements

You can also group keywords for different campaigns and reorder them after an experiment day of displaying advertisements. Note down the performance of the ads, spend more money on successful ads, and stop promoting bad performing advertisements.

In the next section, we will discuss prioritizing the keyword sets for successful evaluations and results.

5) Prioritize

In the final stage of the keyword usage, you need to prioritize the good working keywords for your niche. Sometimes keywords with very high search volume will also have very fewer clicks on the link and a lot fewer sales than you have anticipated. This is the reason why you need to evaluate these ad sets every day and understand the audience and their demographics.

For example, many people search for juice maker but there will be very fewer sales as the audience here is less fierce about the niche. However, consider the keyword geyser. Here the keyword is essential for daily household purposes during winter so this keyword will have more sales.

Prioritizing is important for letting go of things that are not working out for you. It does not make sense to sell products with losses. Even though if you have spent a lot of time preparing and outsourcing a product let go of it if it is not performing well after prioritizing.

In the next section, we will discuss a PPC strategy that can be used for all the PPC campaigns. This strategy is curated from the interviews of many successful FBA inversions. Follow along to know it!

PPC ad strategy

1) Create an automatic ad campaign from the amazon central for your listing

Amazon offers two types of advertisement campaigns in seller central. One of them is an automatic ad campaign where amazon automatically looks out the profitable keywords and advertise for you. Another one is the manual ad campaign where you need to manually insert the keywords that you choose to.

In the seller central go to campaigns, click on the start of an advertisement campaign, and select the automatic ad campaign to start it. You need to enter a budget amount and period for the campaign. For better results spend 25$ initially for a day for seven days on an automatic campaign. Make sure that your product satisfies all the A9 algorithm rules for better and accurate results.

2) Set a fixed budget for 1 week

Remember that Amazon does not ask you to enter the bidding amount for the automatic ad campaigns. Your budget that is 25$, for example, is equally divided between different seed keywords of the product you are listing. Amazon even considers your descriptions and specifications to cater to some profitable keywords and use them to display advertisements.

3) After 1 week stop the campaign and analyse the ad results

After running out the advertisements on an automatic ad campaign for 1 week stop for a while and analyse the results that have come. You need to download the advertisement results by clicking on the export results button.

4) Find the most profitable products and note them down in a separate spreadsheet

After looking at the results, you can find out the profitable keywords that have been doing well. Give the priority to the sales metric and the next to the volume metric. List out all the good keywords in a spreadsheet.

5) Using the profitable keywords create long-tail keywords for your product and start manual ad campaigns

After collecting the keywords, you need to use those keywords to form some of the long-tail keywords. Long-tail keywords are essential to grabbing some significant sales. Brainstorm and form good long-tail keywords and search their volume in a keyword research tool like SEMrush. After a quick search finds the best keywords and uses them for creating manual ad campaigns.

6) Resume both automatic and manual ad campaigns and reduce the budget for automatic

After selecting out the good keywords from your analysis start creating a different set of individual manual campaigns and resume your last automatic ad campaign. Fix your budget and start the campaigns and look at the sales grow.

7) Repeat this and increase your ad sets consistently according to the sales

If you are making good sales try to increase your ad campaigns and budget. You can also experiment with some of the seed keywords with good video advertisements.

8) Stop campaigns, which are underperforming after the good market, run and estimate the profits

If you notice any decreases in the sales or bad Asset performance, you can delete those campaigns. After the end of all the campaigns count out your profits.

This is the best PPC ad strategy that can be applied for any amazon product. Experiment yourselves to learn better about keyword research.

By this, we have completed a brief chapter that delves into complex topics such as keyword research and pays per click ads for amazon. In the next chapter, we will discuss shipping procedures that need to be taken care of to decrease the shipping time. Let us go!

Chapter 6: Tips for the fast shipping process

Start As we already know that Amazon's FBA seller's main priority is to deliver goods using Amazon's efficient logistics system. Amazon has many warehouses all around the world with robots and human labour working tirelessly for delivering products. Amazon also collaborates with hundreds of courier partners to deliver goods from warehouses to customer's shipping addresses. There are many things that go on in a delivery process and it is important to know this information as a seller. In this chapter, we will discuss the shipping process in detail and give some strategies for reducing the delivery time thus making customers happy. Let us go!

For a better understanding of the topic, we will divide the following content into two sections as follows:

a) FBA operating procedure
b) Important points to note for FBA shipment

Let us start discussing the Amazon fulfillment operating rules and regulations in detail as a layman explanation.

a) FBA operating procedure

The operating procedure is a basic blueprint about how things are done at Amazon warehouses and fulfillment centres. Our first step is to send products to the Amazon warehouses.

1) Send the products to Amazon without delay
A seller should know that the shipments should be sent to one of the nearest amazon warehouses. Use perfect labelling and scan it with a wireless barcode scanner before sending it to the warehouses from one of Amazon's delivery partners. When your shipment reaches Amazon warehouse you will receive a tracking message that verifies your product arrival. It stays in those warehouses until an order is placed. If you have very fewer orders you may need to pay additional fees for storing the products in warehouses for more than the estimated time.

2) Amazon pick and pack service
When Amazon receives a successful order from the customer, they start working on the packaging of the goods. Amazon uses sealed packaging systems so that the product does not undergo any damage during the packing procedures. You can file a complaint on Amazon if there is any mishandling of your products. The customer address will be labelled on the shipment and is now all set for the shipment to start shipping.

3) Amazon delivery

Amazon uses various shipping algorithms to successfully place the package in one of its huge containers that are used for shipping to other cities or countries. Amazon uses both ship and airways for foreign shipments whereas trucks are used for local shipments. After the successful reaching of the nearest warehouse, the customer delivery partners will deliver them to the addresses given. Amazon is also responsible for any customer return/exchange requests. All these requests will be handled by the courier partners and take very little time. In the next section, we will discuss some important details that needed to be looked upon and the invoices that should be prepared. Follow along!

Invoices and further procedures for shipping

Whenever you are shipping the products to amazon warehouses, it is important to make invoices for the quantity of the products so that you can crosscheck the charges that are processed by Amazon.

a) Enter the quantity
Open a spreadsheet and enter the order number along with the quantity of the shipment. You need to prepare an FBA calculator using Microsoft excel to automatically calculate the cost based on the quantity. If you are not comfortable with

Microsoft Excel, you can use the invoice tool in the seller central for calculating the costs.

b) Prepare products

After the calculations are, done to prepare the shipments and place them in a container with bubble wraps for sensitive products and glass items. Always follow the amazon packing procedures. If you are not aware of packaging, you can hire amazon workers for completing the packing procedures of course with a stimulated price.

c) Label products

After the shipments are packed, you need to label the products with the barcode of your seller account and scan with a wireless barcode scanner. It is mandatory to scan the label before sending it to the Amazon warehouses. Also, label the products neatly without any wear and tear. Many products will be later sealed by amazon's secured packaging program.

d) Review shipments

If you are satisfied with the packing and are, ready to send the shipments to the amazon warehouses once again review all the shipments and hand them to the truck drivers or your delivery partners. Amazon does not provide shipping from your shipping address to warehouses so make sure that you find a way to send your shipments.

With this, we have given a complete description of the shipping procedures and the processes that need to be handled. In the next section, we will discuss making the shipping process easy for international shipments.

Making the shipping procedure easy for the foreign shipments

Domestic shipping is taken care of Amazon FBA seller program and if your products need to be outsourced from your own country, it makes your work easy. However, if you are importing the products from foreign countries like China it takes a lot more time to outsource and send them to Amazon warehouses. We will in this section discuss the differences between domestic shipping and international shipping in detail. We will also give some strategies to decrease the shipping time if you are importing products from a Chinese supplier.

Differences between Domestic shipping and international shipping

In this shipping procedure, you send the products to warehouses directly using your delivery system. From then Amazon ships them to the customers' addresses.

International shipping
First, you need to receive these shipments from one of the nearby ports and quality check them using various use-cases. All imported products are sent to the customs department for the clearance of those goods. Until the federal authorities issue a no-objection certificate you are not allowed to transport those shipments. After the clearance, all the products need to be sent to the nearest warehouses by yourself, as amazon is not responsible for it.

How to reduce time in international shipping?

International shipping is often considered difficult because it deals with more complications from the customs department in both the Chinese and United States ports. Here is the systematic process that goes on with products coming from international warehouses. We will also mention some strategies to reduce the shipping time to the consumer.

1) When the manufacturer completes the packing of products of your desired units, they are sent to amazon international warehouses in China and stored for a couple of days until the clearance certificate is given for the imports. Make sure there are no illegal products as it may lead to trouble for everyone involved.

2) When the shipment reaches the US ports you or one of your subordinates should make verification with the customs to send it to the nearest Amazon warehouse or your inventory.

3) To reduce the costs of double transportation work with a trusted manufacturer who does not compromise the quality of the product and send those shipments coming from international warehouses directly to the domestic warehouses. From then, the delivery process goes on as normal as the other deliveries.

4) Return shipping will take more time than the domestic shipments as they need to be sent back by you from your inventory to the Chinese manufacturer by express mail after receiving them from the nearest Amazon warehouse. It is better to use the airways option for return products as it takes less time.

Types of shipping methods

a) By waterways

This is the usual method of shopping and costs a little less than the other method. However, the difficult thing is to go on a person to the ports and handling them all by yourself.

b) By airways

It is an easy method to maintain and takes less time to ship the product. However, it costs a little bit more than the usual delivery charges. If you are shipping a high number of units then it is better to depend on airways.

Things to remember for faster shipping

a) Get ready with all the paperwork

It may be frustrating sometimes to let your stock stay in the ports until customs cleared it with no objection certificate. Whenever you are receiving a shipment, prepare all the shipment way before with all the invoices and import certification from the manufacturers. Show the product invoices with the name of your limited liability company for faster processing of procedures.

b) Know what you can import

US authorities prohibit various sensitive materials like drugs to be imported from China. Many health-related products are not allowed to import if they do not compile with the US guidelines. Go to the website of the customs department to download a spreadsheet that gives information about the products that cannot be imported. It is a good practice to check US import guidelines for every product you are trying to import from Chinese suppliers.

c) Never ship counterfeiting products

American authorities have a strict restriction on counterfeiting products nowadays due to the increase in the fraud business model that many sellers have adopted. Even though you are asking for a genuine product sometimes you may get into a situation where the manufacturer has sent you counterfeiting products.

Therefore, a thorough manual checking is necessary whenever your shipments reach the port and if you find any wrong shipments contact your seller and send back those defected products. Never try to make money with counterfeiting products even though it brings larger profits as it can make your business be dissolved when caught by the customs department.

By this, we have completed a brief description of the shipment procedures that are needed to be learned by an Amazon FBA seller. In the next chapter, you will learn about many marketing tactics to promote your products. Follow along to know more about them.

Chapter 7: Advanced marketing strategies to drive sales

Start Marketing is an essential skill and a major cause that brings up sales. It is said that even a bad product can be sold out with good marketing. We are not suggesting you manufacture a bad product, but we are insisting you to develop good marketing skills to increase your product sales cumulatively.

A lot of Amazon FBA sellers rely on Ads for marketing their products and a lot of them are not smart enough to master the art of free marketing tactics that can bring a good number of sales. In this chapter, we will look at both paid and free marketing tactics that can be used by amazon FBA sellers to increase visitors to their listings. Follow carefully and experiment with your product listings. Let us go!

Why is marketing essential?

A lot of visitors search and research for a product before they buy in real. When they find a good blog post or intriguing ad with images, they decide to buy that product. Marketing is essentially getting the right customers to your product page. Targeting ads to demography who have no interest in your products is a waste of time and resources. We will divide this marketing section into three sections namely amazon PPC ads, social networking ads, and miscellaneous strategies. We will first start with Amazon PPC ads that have a good conversion rate.

Amazon PPC ads

If you ever did shop on amazon, you might have seen sponsored ads above the top results whenever you search for a product. These advertisements are called Amazon PPC advertisements where PPC is roughly defined as pay per click. All these advertisements can be started from amazon seller central with the help of bidding on keywords.

What is pay per click?

Pay per click is an advertising method that has become popular due to its enormous potential to bring the users to the product page. In this advertising model, an advertiser needs to pay the money only when the ad is clicked by the user. Other social networking platforms use an advertising model called PPM where an advertiser needs to pay the platforms based on impressions (most likely 1000). The advantage of the PPC advertising model is that the potential views of the product page increases and can result in organic growth if there are positive reviews and feedback after driving the sales due to advertising.

What are the different types of sponsored ads?

Sponsored ads can be displayed in different ways by the amazon curation department. We will look at some of these in detail here.

a) By keywords
The most popular way is by bidding on keywords. Amazon seller central helps you to select the keywords you want to target on in their portal and then start the campaign for a time interval. For example, if you have selected the keyword washing machine in your campaign, they whenever a potential user searches with the same keyword you are listing will be displayed as a sponsored ad. The conversion rate is usually high for these ads because consumers believe in Amazon's top results and a lot of them will not even notice the sponsored tag besides the listing.

b) Headline ads
If you are a seller who has more than one product, you can purchase ad space to display all of them at one time. These

types of ads are called headline ads and are displayed on the top page with intriguing images. If done carefully these types of ads can drive sales very quickly.

c) In other product pages

Whenever a visitor is checking through a product page amazon recommends sponsored products on the side. There is a huge chance of visitors clicking on the links if they are of the same category and less price. However, it costs a little bit more money as people often do not notice these ads.

d) Off-site advertisements

Amazon and other e-commerce platforms usually use cookies to track their user past information. That is when someone visits an amazon product page cookie stores it and displays the same product pages as advertisements in other websites via google or Bing ads. Amazon uses huge marketing algorithms to display off-site advertisements. Therefore, if you ever see your ads on other websites is not panicked because it is Amazon that is trying to increase your sales via off-site marketing methods

e) Via email newsletters

Emails are one of the most effective mediums to target users. Amazon collects a ton of email information and details specific to the user and sends sponsored products via newsletters based on their past experiences. You can opt-out of these options when you are buying ad spaces. It is not so effective compared to others because many users consider amazon emails as marketing spam and ignore them. Therefore, experiment with your own risk with Amazon sponsored newsletters.

Why advertisements should be done?

Many sellers might get doubts about advertisements as just a quick way for amazon to spin out money from their partners. However, research done by search engine optimization firms suggests that successful ad campaigns can help to increase the organic search growth. In addition, advertisements can help you understand the market trend and helps you to choose the best products for selling.

How advertisements can increase organic rankings?

Advertisements can directly influence sales. If you can get a good number of sales in a stipulated time, then your sales velocity increases and amazon algorithm prefer you are higher from other products. Therefore, it is indeed true that advertisements drive sales and increases your sales. Although you are also prone to bad reviews and a decrease in search ranking if, your product is of low quality. So, decide whether your product is of good quality and if it is necessary to promote it with advertisements.

Is it worth trying the Amazon PPC?

Amazon PPC has been a success mantra for sellers from the past few years. The best thing about Amazon PPC is you can regulate the timings of the advertisements and can monitor them in a way such that they can be published for certain demographics and keywords. You need to experiment with different campaigns at first to determine the winning ad set. Amazon does all of these said with the Automatic PPC ad campaign. It divides your keywords into different ad sets and selects the best performing advertisement automatically using their platforms. If you are good at judging the analytics, you can use a custom PPC ad campaign. As per records, Amazon PPC usually drives your sales by 33% making it a worthy investment for Amazon FBA sellers.

Amazon advertising costs

Amazon advertisers cost a little less than their counterparts Google and Facebook did. Facebook uses impressions model to calculate whereas google ad sets are often overcrowded making the prices high. With Amazon, you can maintain your campaign prices as per the performance and target as many keywords as you can at one time. It is better to stick to niche keywords at first and later experiment with the long-tail keywords with lower visitors.

Bidding method

Just like you, many Amazon sellers are willing to advertise with Amazon for selling these products. For this reason, ad spaces are given for a keyword using a bidding method. When you are selecting an ad space for a root keyword, you need to enter the minimum bidding amount of your choice. If you are lucky, you will be allotted with that ad space or otherwise, you need to retry with an increased bidding price. If you are not sure about bidding, you can select the automatic amazon bidding option, which selects the price in a way that you will be allotted with the ad space. It is important to understand thoroughly the concept of bidding while advertising for saving small amounts of money.

Social networking ads

Social networking websites are the most used websites nowadays by every individual. Many Amazon sellers spend money to display PPC ads on social media networking platforms. In this section, we will discuss a new advertisement strategy called remarketing using social networks.

What is remarketing?

Imagine that someone visits your product page and adds into the cart but did not check out the order for whatever reason it may be. All the processing information of the visitor will be stored in the cookies of his browser. Amazon inserts these cookies to display advertisements by different third-party tracking cookies. When you use this third-party cookie, social networks will track all the required users who visited your website as all of them consist of the same cookie information.

Is remarketing a good strategy?

Remarketing is a very good strategy to increase your sales by offering some coupon codes for these last-minute quitters. You can also use various third-party software to monitor your remarketing campaigns. Remarketing ad campaigns consist of a new ad space called PPS, where it stands for pay for sale. You will only be charged when a visitor places an order. However, the charges for PPS are a little bit high than the other advertisements.

In the below section we will describe different known strategies for various social media network platforms. Follow along!

1) Facebook

Facebook is well known for displaying advertisements based on the number of impressions. As Facebook has many daily users, it is suggested to use ppm ads. For driving good sales using Facebook ads you need to create good illustrations, images so that the posts will intrigue the Facebook audience, and interact with them increasing your organic reach. In the Facebook post insert your product link with URL shorteners, write good catchy phrases, and make the user click the link and drive into your product page. You can also use Facebook carousel adds if you are trying to market two or more products of yours at one time. Facebook significantly drives a good number of sales when compared to other networks due to its large user base.

2) Instagram

Instagram is a sibling site of Facebook and is mostly an image-sharing website. Instagram users are often considered as the most volatile user base with a lot of interaction but very fewer sales. Make sure that you are placing video ads for better reach of your advertisement. Remarketing is the best strategy to drive sales from Instagram.

3) Pinterest
Pinterest is a platform that is a boon for product marketers as its user base is mostly waiting to buy new products. Pinterest depends on images so invest yourself in making up good brand images of your product using a good camera. Pinterest posts get viral when your pin is shared on other boards. Make sure that your product page URL is inserted in the URL of the pin. Pinterest is best known for carousel images too. Therefore, if you are planning on making ads for multiple products use carousel ads and place all your product images.

4) Reddit
Reddit is called the dark market of the internet and all its user bases are harsh on anyone who does marketing. However, Reddit is the top ninth website in terms of visitors according to Alexa rankings. This makes Reddit a good place for advertisers who are smart and trying to give out some value to the community. Reddit ads are cheap compared to other websites as their user base interacts less with the advertisements.

However, if done well they can be used to drive some sales. Try to ask Redditor's thoughts about your pockets in a popular subreddit that is relevant to your category and ask them their suggestions to improve the product more and place a link for them. If people are hooked up with the product, you may get some organic sales without spending any money.

5) Twitter

Twitter is a social media network that primarily runs with the help of hashtags and offers very less post content (280 characters). Twitter is a good place to push your ads to like-minded people of your niche. Collect the popular hashtags belonging to your niche and use them whenever you are trying to tweet so that your organic reach increases. Do not try to be like selling a product but act as if you are giving information to the twitter users. You can also promote ppm ads using twitter for significantly lower prices. Use Twitter automating tools to fill your twitter feed with your listings.

With these social media marketing techniques, you can increase your sales and thus your sales velocity and finally your search result rank. You can also experiment with other networks and WhatsApp marketing to increase your domestic sales. The sky is the limit for experimentation in marketing. Try some of your ways.

In the next section, we will discuss some miscellaneous marketing techniques that are favoured by successful Amazon FBA sellers. Follow along!

Miscellaneous marketing techniques

1) Surveys

Surveys are an easy way to know what your customers are expecting from your niche. You can fill out a survey with your options and submit them in survey websites like survey monkey where you need to pay money for successful survey completion. You can market these survey links in other social networks and collect enough valid information about the expectations of your niche audience and can use this information to find new profitable and people liking products. Surveys will help your audience in a better way and can help you improve your positive reviews.

2) Competitive analysis

Competitive analysis is one of the most underrated methods of all the marketing methods that are used. It is underrated because people do not understand the influence and impact of it. Look at factors like the build quality of the product and packaging to understand why people are satisfied with the product. Look whether they included any help sheets for the users to handle the product.

Look at the marketing strategies they have followed using different SEO tools like Moz and Semrush. Google also provides the ad money spent by publishers if their campaign names are entered. After successfully gathering information using competitive analysis use, this data to build an excellent product that can drive quick sales with positive reviews.

3) Reverse engineering

Reverse engineering is a marketing and seller skill that needs to be used by sellers for successfully grabbing the pie of the e-commerce market. Reverse engineering deals with ordering your competitor's products and researching their whereabouts and manufacturing locations. You can estimate a price for the manufacturing of the product if you hold the product in person.

Reverse engineering also deals with advertisements by your competitors. There are few third-party services like jungle scout that help you to look at the advertisements of your products which can help you get an overall understanding of the tactics they are being used for promotions. Reverse engineering is a good skill and can be applied in every stage of the product development if done smartly.

You can follow some of the black hat forums to understand the tactics they follow to know information about a successful product. Reverse engineering strategy works well if you are in the apparel industry and are looking for new models. There are software's like those that tee estimator that does this job for you automatically if a keyword is given.

4) email-list building

The pre-launch period is one of the most important phases for product success. Pre-launch marketing should be done for quickly grabbing the top sellers rank in its initial stages. Amazon prefers new products that are performing well and even boost their search engine rankings by 200%. If your product is huge, successful amazon sponsors them in their newsletters for driving more sales. To make pre-launch marketing effective you need to collect good e-mail list months before the product release.

E-mail listing is a very effective marketing technique to collect your niche audience by offering them some valuable resources. Maintain a website on your own or sponsor a post about your product in one of your niche's popular websites. Mail Chimp is one of the famous e-mail marketing tools to send emails to your listing emails with resources depending on their past surveys answered. Before your product launch, you can send an email with coupon codes exclusively for your email-listing members and can drive some initial sales. Remember to not send many emails in a day and act professionally with your members.

5) Giveaways and contests

Giveaways and contests are the other pioneer marketing methods that can be used to increase positive reviews on your listing. Conduct a contest on your website or your social media pages and giveaway a few products to the desired winners. Ask them to share their reviews on the product page as a mark of appreciation for you. However, do not force winners to post reviews as it may lead to a negative influence on you as a seller.

You can start contests or quizzes on your website using third-party tools like Viralsweep and king sumo. These third-party premium tools help to increase page reach of your product pages by automatically sharing your product link on the contestant's social media networks. Conduct different giveaway contestants for your e-mail listing members and collect audience emails while organizing contests.

6) Kickstarter

Although not being a marketing strategy Kickstarter strategy is used for letting like-minded people know the good work you are doing. Kickstarter is a crowdfunding platform that lets you share your innovative product idea and get funding. Make sure that you are using this strategy only if you are trying to mass-produce an innovative product that serves a good purpose for your niche audience.

If you are just trying to spinoff an already famous product for crowdfunding, then you are going to get a lot of black lash from the crowdfunding community. If people find your product innovative, they will fund you some money for the manufacturing procedures. Post the protocols and a brief description of your product with a presentation video to gather more funds.

7) Amazon promotions as deal sites

Amazon offers an amazon associate program for its affiliate markets to drive sales in the e-commerce platform. Amazon offers commissions varying from 4% to 10% on different categories. Amazon associate program is one of the most successful affiliate programs on the internet as it tracks the information using cookies method. However, cookies stay alive only for 24 hours due to excessive competition.

Amazon FBA sellers can issue coupons and send them to popular amazon associates in your niche via email/ social network. These coupons help them earn extra commission from your product and will help your listing to drive more sales due to their promotions and reviews.

There are also many coupons sharing websites like couponmania.com where users share coupons for other visitors. Uploading your coupons with good discounts can land you some sales from these websites. In initial stages, every sale does count so make sure you are registered with some popular coupon sharing platforms.

8) Automated follow-up emails

Automated emails are an easy way to get some good leads. We can use the software as if mail champ to send automatically to follow up emails with the help of tracking cookies that amazon uses. In the automated follow-up emails, you can send coupon codes exclusively for the customers to lure them into buying your products. This strategy is a remarketing strategy that is often successful and costs less.

9) Creating a sales funnel

A sales funnel is a smart way to sell your products on amazon. However, you need to create a website using third-party tools like those that click funnels to implement the magic of funnel marketing system. In the funnel system, you do not try to sell a product at first, but you give valuable information to the visitor and collect his email address.

In addition, moving further we give him very useful information about the micro-niche and cleverly trick him into buying our products to make use of that knowledge. A sales funnel needs time to build upon and you need to work very hard to market your website. Remember that the funnel technique is complex and can help you learn more about your niche audience and their tastes. This experience will help you in making good products in the future.

10) Off-site advertising

This is a classical way of telling people that you are selling a product. Off-site advertising readily means giving advertisements on search engines. You can rely both on Google and on Bing for advertisements as they both have some good user base. If you are starting with less budget, you can experiment with Bing as they give a 100$ trail ad account.

11) Offline marketing techniques

Amazon users are not always online. You can use classical marketing techniques like distributing flyers and conducting workshops to spread a word mouth about your product. If Offline marketing is not working, then just let go of it and invent your marketing techniques. That is what a good marketer does. Invent and Innovate.

By this, we have completed a brief chapter about marketing your amazon FBA business using various tactics and techniques. I hope that you have learned a lot of valid information and in the next chapter; we will start learning about the techniques to find profitable products. Let us go!

Chapter 8: How to find profitable products?

Start Finding profitable products is an essential skill to stay alive in the market. Selling products that no one is willing to buy is a bad idea. You need to understand the demographics of the niche/category that you are trying to focus on and use that demographic information to research the specific interesting products they might like. This research process is often hectic and sometimes even takes weeks for coming up with a good product idea. In the next section, we will discuss some proven ways that can be used to find profitable products. Let us go!

a) Check from amazon associates

Many profitable products are being promoted by thousands of amazon associates by their blogs and websites. All you need to do is found out the popular blogs and websites in your niche using tools like Moz and scrape all the amazon links they are pointing out to. Many third-party applications help you to scrape out the amazon links within a click on a website.

After careful study of the links, pointing out to you can conclude the successful or popular products they are trying to promote to their visitors for a commission. Note down all the popular products and list out them in a spreadsheet and compare all the specifications they are using. This is a classical way of finding profitable products using the Amazon associate program.

b) Use Amazon reviews

Amazon reviews are an easy way to understand both the positives and negatives of your niche products. You can look out at the positive products and note down the specifics that the customers have loved. Nevertheless, for finding profitable private labelled products you need to check out the one-star reviews of the popular products in your niche. All the one-star reviews will leave out a note about the disappointment of the product. You can find some valuable information about what your niche audience is expecting? In addition, you can use this information to develop new profitable products.

c) Find products with fewer customer reviews

We already knew from past chapters that customer reviews are the most important metric considered by the Amazon A9 algorithm to let the keywords rank in the SERP. For this sublime reason, you need to find out products within your category that has very fewer customer reviews and compete with them to rank faster. Products with fewer customer reviews should contain a root keyword that belongs to your product. If you are lucky, you will find a couple of products and mix them so that they can be used as your next product protocol.

d) Use jungle scout to know estimated sales

Jungle scout is one of the famous amazon third-party service tools that monitors all your listings and display analytics for better monitoring. Amazon jungle scout also offers a plugin that can constantly monitor your competitor's sales and display that information for you. It is an accurate number but an estimated number using complex algorithms that jungle scout possesses. You will find some valuable information about viral products with sales in your category. You can also come up with a pricing strategy after looking at all the data. In this way, by using a jungle scout sales estimator you can find some of the profitable product categories to sell.

e) Test products yourself by a website

To find whether a product is profitable or not you need to check it by yourself. Order your competitor products and crosscheck those using different industrial methods. Reverse engineer the product to understand the durability and simplicity of the product. Try to analyse a few more competitors and note down all the good features. Using these good features develop a new prototype for a private label product or search for a product in the foreign industries and retailers that offers all the features that you have noted down.

f) Don't sell products that belong to big brands

Amazon is a pretty competitive place regardless of the big competitors. Big competitors are already successful Amazon partners and always try to hold their position. For example, in the smartphone industry, Apple and Samsung are pioneers. If you try to sell a product or accessories in this category, it is very difficult to make yourself get a top rank due to these big brand names. Moreover, customers will also prefer to choose brand names instead of you for their needs. Therefore, it is foolish to compete with brands (that are keywords they rank for) that are very popular and trustworthy in your niche.

g) Use Google ads to know about ads

Google collects a bunch of user information and advertising data for further evaluation or marketing purposes. Few third-party services scrape the google advertising systems to list out the ads placed by a publisher. With this strategy, you can find out the keywords that your competitors are trying to rank using advertisements. It is worth looking at all those golden keywords for innovating a new viral product.

h) See best sellers and research

A good way to find profitable products is by checking out the top seller products in your category and subcategories. Amazon jungle scout offers a plugin that lets you scrap all the bestseller products in your category on a click. You can export that information to a spreadsheet and analyse those using metrics to find a profitable product that can give you a good profit. Before trying to commit with a product do hard research and the seller prices, resources and manufacturers for a brief estimation of capital that you need for starting the product sales.

I) look at the buyers and stop chasing through abandoned niches

Amazon almost consists of products from every category. However, only some niches are considered to be good at driving adequate sales. Many people try to sell products in a niche where people are less likely to buy. This is the reason why you should check the estimated sales metric using third-party services to conclude whether your niche audiences are good buyers or not. If you find out that, your niche audience is not buying products then it is better to stop your resources and time on it and start focusing on a golden niche where people buy products. Health, furniture, pet care is some of the examples of golden niches in an E-commerce platform.

j) Use historical sales data

A few third-party tools provide you the estimated quarterly sales for every category and sub-category. Amazon publishes this information for proofing liability to its shareholders. With this historical sales data, you can estimate whether a niche is having good sales or not. Historical sales data can also be used to think about a price policy depending on the behaviour of the niche audience.

Advanced tricks to become profitable with Amazon FBA business

In this section, we will discuss some of the proven strategies that can be used to increase your Amazon FBA sales. Remember that these are curated from the interviews of successful amazon FBA sellers.

1) Join FBA forums and update daily with information

A lot of FBA sellers' experiment with a lot of seller central tools and implement different strategies to drive out sales. Amazon FBA sellers are very much happy to give back to the community in FBA forums and via websites. Join one of those web forums and constantly check the popular posts so that you are not missing any advanced strategies and tricks that other FBA sellers are using. While using forums you will also find some of the innovative marketing strategies, which you can implement for your listings, and product launches.

2) Bandit app

Always use third party seller applications to get a good understanding of the analytics of your sales. People often find it difficult to find patterns of success in their business. When looking at the graphical analytical charts of your listings you can easily find out where your sales are coming from. You can use this data to further outsource the most selling categories and products. A third-party application called Bandit is very intriguing and can help you further enhance your monitoring skills. You can also use amazon seller apps in your smartphones, which displays some of the basic charts of your business.

3) Never try to cheat the platform, follow rules

Amazon is a pirate land and if you want to be one of those pirates, it is understandable. Nevertheless, it is important to say you that cheating the platform will only land you into trouble at the end of the race. So, always get yourselves filled with the amazon rules and regulations. Try to read new rules that amazon brings up from its weekly newsletters. Follow blogs and websites to completely understand the rules of this most trusted e-commerce company. You can even look at the dark side of the amazon using black hat SEO blogs. But only use that knowledge to defend from spammers and counterfeiters.

4) Become a shopper. Understand buyers' philosophy

If you want to become a good seller, you need to be aware of your buyers. There is nothing stupider than trying to sell a product that you do not like using. Always try to think like a consumer when you are trying to start a listing. Use different online shopping platforms and try to understand what the consumers are expecting in your niche. Read negative reviews of other products in your category and understand why they are not satisfied with that product. Try to implement those features and specifications that users are expecting in your product. As the saying goes "To become a good seller you need to be a good buyer first".

5) Distribute coupon codes. Create an email list

Amazon offers discount coupon codes to be generated by the seller on the seller platform. You can use these coupon codes to distribute it by yourself or send it to amazon associates using email newsletters. Coupon codes are a good way of attracting customers to check out the product.

A significant decrease in the product can make may consumers press that "buy" button. Nevertheless, always make sure that you are not cutting out many of your profits by using your coupon codes. Nevertheless, remember that high sales are important for a listing in its initial stages and after that organic search will constantly bring you good profits.

6) Expand your business

Few Amazon FBA sellers start well on the platform but gradually loses on the sales when they stop outsourcing and expanding their business further. It is always essential to increase your business when the right time comes. You need to improve your negotiation skills with manufacturers for designing better products. Experiment with different categories and niches and start giving advertisements on various social media platforms. If you are on sole proprietorship, start shifting to a private liable company for various advantages. Expanding is always tough but it means it. So, try to dream big especially when you are in an industry that has huge potential.

7) Reinvest your profits do not save them

When one of your product listings goes viral, you will start getting profits. Use a good portion of those profits to reinvest in other products. Experiment with different products in the same niche and start producing your viral product in different variants. Make a video advertisement with freelance artists to target Instagram and Pinterest audience. Try to think out of the box with your budget and double your profits.

8) Stop selling lower-priced products. Believe me, it is not worth it

Amazon has all kinds of products from cheap materials to rich products. A lot of sellers try to sell products at fewer prices for very fewer profits. Many of these products are either from local retailers or from Chinese suppliers. The reason I am saying you do not depend on these lower-priced products is that there is no scope for expanding the business with fewer prices.

If you want to make higher profits you need to start selling your products called Private labelled products rather than selling the same products that everyone sells. (We have a section detailing the strategy to sell private labelled products in the last chapter. Read it for further information)

9) Perfect your product pages

Product pages are the most important way to drive sales. Make sure they are of high quality. Use freelancers to design illustrations and insert them into your product pages. Write clear-cut descriptions and specifications for your product in a way that keywords are inserted for good search engine ranking. If you have, a good budget tries to make a video about your product, which can be further used for Instagram ads too. If you are not comfortable with video cameras, you can hire freelancers to make the product videos for you. It costs less and drives a lot of attention than traditional advertisements.

10) Make bundles and sell bundled products at fewer prices

Amazon offers its sellers to sell their products using bundled offers. Bundled offers are usually of low cost than their prices and offer the same shipping time. Always bundle the right set of products for good reach over your niche audience. You can even collaborate with other sellers to sell your product and theirs. However, packaging may be a little bit difficult if you are trying to send both of them at once. Make sure that you have enough inventory to sell bundled products before updating the listings. You can stop the offer whenever you need to just by a click on amazon seller central.

11) Start selling private labelled products

Private labelled products are the best strategy to earn easy money. It means that you are selling a product under your brand name so that you can easily crack the buy box in amazon's top results. Private labelled products need good research and competitor analysis to crack the jackpot. We will discuss in detail about private labelled products in the subsequent chapters.

12) Crush your competitor sales with fewer prices

Sometimes you need to act smart and start reducing your prices during the amazon black market sales. If you are selling 50 units per day and earning an 800$ profit every day you need to start thinking about selling 100 units with fewer prices and earning 1200$ profit a day. It sometimes makes sense to compete with your competitors and earn the top result by gathering high sales. We already discussed the impact of sales velocity on the amazon algorithm and a little bit more sales with less pricing can help to increase your organic reach.

13) Find profitable replenishable products

Replenishable products are the ones that are always in the stock in any part of the year. These are the classic products and people buy them at every part of the year irrespective of seasons. Get a brainstorm list of these products and store them in your inventory for the rest of the year. Nevertheless, them in bulk so that you will get good bucks as profit at the end of the year.

14) Stop the listing if it is not doing well

Many people spend most of their profits on marketing and advertising listings that are not making any money. It is very hard to let go of a product that you have researched and made hard work to reproduce them into the real world.

15) Wait for Christmas

Every year during Christmas amazon sells products more than any time in the year. Get ready about the shopping season and make sure that your inventory is full and is of full stock. Introduce coupons to sell all your stock within very less time. You need to invest well in buying products that are important during a holiday season. A good Christmas season will help you gain more profits than all the other seasons combined.

In this chapter, we have given a good explanation for finding profitable products in the first section with several good strategies. In the next section, we discussed some of the advanced tricks to make your FBA business grow successfully without any limitations. With this, we have completed the most basic part of our book and in our next chapter; we will discuss defending yourself from counterfeiting and some of the legal topics that an FBA seller needs to be aware of. Follow along!

Chapter 9: Getting rid of Project hijackers

Start Amazon is a very large e-commerce platform and is sometimes heaven for spammers and product hijackers for various reasons it is weak at. As we said already, Amazon's main motive is to satisfy its customers and increase its quarterly sales. Amazon is often criticized for doing very little to nothing to stop spammers and counterfeiters from ruining the e-commerce platform.

A multinational company like Amazon can easily invest in Developing machine learning and data mining algorithms that can automatically detect counterfeiting products and ban their seller accounts. Nevertheless, whatever the reasons maybe Amazon is nowhere near to making these dreams possible and is making sellers to actively monitor their listings and reporting those counterfeiting products to the Amazon feedback team. In this chapter, we will discuss strategies that can be implemented to defend yourself from product hijackers who lower your profits. Let us go!

What is listing hijacking?

Let me explain this to you in a layman example. Imagine that you have started selling a private label product called "Double juice maker" after a ton of research and negotiating with your manufacturers. Your product got a tremendous response and was received well by customers with positive reviews and feedback. You are making roughly 50 sales a day consistently and one day you find out that the sales are decreasing constantly for some unknown reason.

You are worried and after a quick research on your listing, you find out that someone is selling the same product at less price. After thorough research, you have found out that some counterfeiter is selling your exact product manufactured from Chinese sellers at a lesser price and this is affecting your sales. Apart from losing your sales due to the reason that your counterfeiter is selling a cheap product, your listing is pouring out with negative reviews and if this goes on your product will stop getting any sales in the future. This exact process of hijacking your sales with counterfeiting is known as product hijacking.

As now, you are aware of the situation we will now discuss various strategies that can be used to defend from the pirates of the Amazon e-commerce platform. Follow along!

1) Contact the seller directly

Whenever you find out that your product has been counterfeited you need to send a formal email to the listing owner. You can find his email address on the seller page or you can just find it out on the product page on the left side. Make a good formal email that says that you are not interested to work it out in a hard way. Give a deadline for the seller to remove the listing and warn him that if he is not doing that within the deadline, he is liable to legal charges both from Amazon and from you.

Also, attach the link and the product images to make sure that you are the owner of the listing. Wait for at least 48 hours to receive an email from him or constantly check whether the listing has been removed or not. If the listing is still live after 48 hours, you need to send a complaint to the amazon as they have very strict counterfeiting rules if you report the links.

2) File a complaint with Amazon

Visit the amazon feedback page and select the option that says Amazon anti-counterfeiting policy. In the email that you are sending mention your problem in detail and give the links to your original listing and the counterfeiting one. Send high-quality images of both yours and the product hijackers so that the feedback team can understand that the anonymous seller has committed counterfeiting.

If you are confused, please look at the amazon help section that says about the terms and conditions related to counterfeiting claims. After a quick check amazon will remove the listing on its own and will warn the FBA seller if it is of the first time or will ban the seller from the platforms if they have found out that the seller has been trying to cheat the platform constantly.

3) Register with Amazon brand registry

To make sure that these mishaps do not happen in the future you need to be registered with the Amazon brand registry so that your listing will get a badge of your brand, which can make product hijackers back down. You need to select a catchy brand name for your product and input a mandatory website of your brand. So, make sure you create a modern website with additional information about your product. However, registering in the brand registry does not completely make your escape from counterfeiters. This is just an added protection mechanism that you need to get aware of.

4) Brand your products with images

Images are the most intriguing part of the product page both for buyers and for counterfeiters. A lot of the product hijackers send your images as prototypes for the Chinese suppliers to make duplicate products of low quality. Therefore, a better solution would be to use images showing your brand name from different sides. This branding projection will remind the counterfeiters of legal problems that they need to face due to project hijacking.

5) Build a website and social network pages

As we said before while registering for the Amazon brand registry a website is mandatory. Create a modern website and fill it with all your product images. Post a page with terms and conditions and make the counterfeiters' policy in bold so that they will be warned. Also, try to maintain different social media accounts and be active in them posting about your products. A counterfeiter will not take risk of hijacking products of the seller who is constantly monitoring and being active in social media. They know that it is not worth it.

6) Monitor constantly

Many Amazon FBA sellers are not keen or interested in monitoring their listing. It is a very wise thing to constantly monitor your sales using a different analytical tool or product management tools. You can find various third-party tools that constantly monitor your listings and send a weekly report. Use mobile apps when you are free to constantly check the sales report and find out why your sales have been decreasing if there is a change in the sales pattern. Attend webinars and workshops that help you improve your monitoring abilities. If you are too busy with shipping and manufacturing hire an amazon virtual assistant to monitor the listings for you.

7) Lower pricing

Whenever you found out that your product has been counterfeited you need to minimize the losses that you are facing. The only approach to stop the counterfeiter from getting any further sales is by reducing your listing price. In this way, you can gather those sales that are being passed on to him due to the low price. Also, try to analyse the pricing analytics closely so that there will not be any problem in the future with the listing. Carefully estimate the sales that you might have lost in a spreadsheet and use it as a motivation to monitor constantly using different third-party tools.

8) Differentiate yourself from others

The only way you can minimize the counterfeiters on your listings is by making your products as unique as possible so that it will become difficult to copy your products. Always use brand names, images, and descriptions that show up your uniqueness. Try to sell private labelled products rather than cheap junk products from wholesale retailers. Differentiating from others is not an easy thing especially when there is heavy competition. So, brainstorm different ideas to be as unique as possible.

9) Ask your friends to buy and then the complaint

Are you worried that amazon has not removed your listing even after your multiple emails being sent? This does not happen often but if you ever face this situation follow the below strategy to make the listing deleted from the Amazon platform.

Step- by step instruction to make the listing get deleted from amazon

a) Send the fake listing to your friend and let him order the product.

b) When the product is received ask him to photograph the product and complaint to amazon from the buyer feedback section.

c) Ask him to insert sentences that completely gives an idea that the product has been counterfeited and ask him to give bad feedback about the product quality.

d) When an Amazon representative looks at the feedback form, he will notice both the listings and will delete the counterfeiting product within 24 hours.

e) You can even use this strategy with a couple of people to get a faster response from the amazon technical team.

10) Amazon hijacker alerts

Multiple third-party tools closely monitor your listings and notify you whenever there is a problem with the listing. You can use software like Jungle scout to get informed without constantly monitoring and killing your productivity. However, these tools will cost you a dime. So, decide whether it is better to buy a third tool or lose on some of your sales. The ball is in your court.

11) Offer products that cannot be produced easily / bundle them

Many Amazon sellers have been counterfeited in the initial stages of the e-commerce platform as there is a very bad response time from the amazon technical team back then. However, things have changed, and Amazon is taking counterfeiting seriously nowadays. Nevertheless, you may wonder even after these regulations why this practice is still going on. The answer is simple, it is easy to make money and people are not often legally charged.

To get rid of these product hijackings some of the most innovative FBA sellers have started creating extremely innovative practices to stop their product from being counterfeited. Here are the two best suggestions that you need to consider the following.

a) Start selling products that are very difficult to counterfeit

Often product hijackers replace the products with cheap Chinese products. However, if you try to irk them with innovation in your products it makes them difficult to exactly copy the counterfeit. It is difficult to counterfeit polished yoga mats than normal yoga mats. So, always try to research well on the private labelled product you are going to sell and patent the rights on it.

b) Start bundling the products

Amazon offers a quick solution to this counterfeiting problem by making you sell bundled products. Try to bundle juice maker with a combination of vegetable mixer for making the counterfeiter's job tougher.

By this, we have completed a brief and thorough explanation about product hijacking and strategies to be used to make your products being safe from being hijacked. In the final section of this book, we will discuss legal issues and a few additional strategies you need to follow when you are in the Amazon FBA business. Follow along to know about it!

a) Accounting

As your business goes, you need to be very aware of the accounts and the business costs that you are entering upon the invoices. Amazon offers few accounting tools in its seller central for faster processing of the sales information. Amazon uses accrual-based accounting, which briefly says that when a product is successfully shipped to the customer the prices automatically add up in your monthly accounting chart.

However, you cannot completely depend on Amazon accounting features because your business costs scale up from manufacturing the product to storing them in your inventory. A lot of tax information needs to be entered if you are a private limited liability company. If your accounting invoices are perfect, then it will be easy to request tax returns from the federal government. For all these reasons, it is important to note down every invoice with accurate costs and revaluate them at every end of the month by yourself. If your business is expanding and if all the taxation is becoming complex for you then you can hire a chartered accountant to look the accounts for you.

b) Receipt management

Receipt management is a practical way to store all your invoices and taxation information in an orderly manner. Collect all the business negotiation emails with the suppliers and print out them along with the manufacturer's invoice for the delivery of the units. You should also print out all the invoices for weekly sold products and place them orderly in racks in a sealed key box in your office. Receipt management is a good way to save some crucial time at tax deadlines.

c) Automatic price changer

This is one of the most used third-party tools for changing the price automatically for your listings. This service gets access to your amazon product listing account and will have the ability to voluntarily reprice the products. The price will be fluctuated according to the rules that have been set up by the user in the portal.

App eagle is one of the famous tools that is used exactly for this purpose. It works effectively and it takes very little time to observe a change.

d) Outsourcing labor's

Outsourcing labours is a clever thing to do if you need to submit many shipments in less time. Packing all the inventory all by yourself is very tough and will not happen at the correct time. Whenever you are faced with this problem, it often happens during holiday seasons when a lot more orders are placed you can hire labour from outsourcing websites such as myfulfilmentteam.com to outsource labours for a temporary period for you. You can look at those charges they take for an hour and outsource as many as labour's you need. Outsourcing is a very smart thing to do and earn suitable profits for your business without any hiccups.

e) Sales tax

This is not a tax-related book, but we will just advise you pay your sales tax on time for facing no problems in the future. Look up at the state tax website to know the percentage of sales tax in your state. Monitor all your transactions and enter them in an online tax form or you can submit on mail to the federal department. You should consult a real accountant before paying the sales tax just for confirmation that you are doing everything right. If everything is right, then you can just pay the taxes online or by wire transfer within a few minutes. Do thorough research about Sales tax via the Internet or meet a tax consultant for further assistance.

By this, we have completed a brief chapter that looked up at many things like counterfeiting, taxation and outsourcing labours. In the next chapter, we will give a short roadmap to private-labelled products. Follow along!

Chapter 10: Roadmap to private labelled products

Start this is a bonus chapter that gives a detailed systematic Amazon business creation using private-labelled products. In the previous chapters of this book, we have already given a little bit of introduction about the private labelled products. In this chapter, we will give a systematic roadmap that will help you make a living with Amazon FBA business. This chapter is designed in such a way that you will revise all the concepts that you have learned in this book.

Layman's explanation of private labelled products

Private labelled products are the products produced by you with a brand name. Your product should not be a rip-off of another successful product but a product with different build models and some changes in the design. You can even add some new features to the successfully selling products to make them like even better liked by the consumers.

Here we explain a fourteen-step strategy to sell private-labelled products. This section explains the roadmap of selling private labelled products from research to dealing with return products. Let us learn about it easily.

Step 1: Looking at the data and finding a good profitable product

We can find many search volume metric data using tools like keyword tool.io and amazon scout. You can even collect data from search engines like google to decide the better keywords that work for your category. Understand the trend of the consumers and decide the idea for a good profitable product.

Step 2: Track all the competitor products and analyze them

If you are ready with the product idea, then you need to dive into the next step and start collecting your competitor products in the same niche. After understanding, the pros and cons of your competitor's product make a roadmap to create a new product that consists of all the good features of your competitors.

Step 3: Creating the product protocol

After understanding and I have come to a conclusion about the specifications such as build quality, material, size and shape of the product try to picture the product in the form of a practical. If you are bad at designing products, you can hire a product prototype to create it for you. If you are interested, you can even create a 3D render for the prototype.

Step 4: Contacting the Chinese suppliers

Now send the protocol to many Chinese suppliers from Alibaba with your specifications and expected quality. Negotiate with them perfectly and offer them a 60% deposit after receiving the trial sample pieces. Pay money for the sample pieces most preferably via wire transfer to Chinese manufacturers.

Step 5: Ordering sample pieces

Within a week or two depending on the shipping procedures, you will get your sample pieces of the products from the suppliers. Check them thoroughly using different quality testing parameters. You can even hire a professional to check the product in-depth and give a report for you. After looking at the products, if you are satisfied you can nod with the supplier to start your business.

Step 6: Place your order with the manufacturer

After verifying, the quality place the order with the manufacturer and pay deposit according to your agreements. When the products are being prepared work hard to create a marketing plan for driving more sales. Look out FBA forums to learn some of the new innovative strategies that other sellers are using.

Step 7: Create a launch list for pre-launch promotions

As your product launch gets sooner start to collect e-mails using different strategies from websites and by funnels. Send these emails with information about your launch product. Offer them a discount price and let them pre-order the products. Pre-orders are a good way to motivate yourselves.

Step 8: Creating and optimizing the listing

After the products have been shipped to your inventory, check the quality and deal with the customs department for clearance. After packaging, the shipments should be sent to amazon warehouses. In addition, when your product reaches the warehouses start the listing and enter all the product details with good illustrations and product images with your brand name showing clearly.

Step 9: Brainstorming about dealing with reviewers

When your listing goes, the life you need to stay focused on the first couple of reviews. Get those good reviews from some of your friends. Make brainstorming ideas to deal with bad reviews. Consider changing prices for different holiday seasons as one of your profit gaining tactics.

Step 10: Getting your first positive reviews

Use different innovative tactics to get your first positive reviews. Reduce the price so that you will drive more sales and increase your sales velocity during the initial days. Offer coupon codes for some very good positive reviews.

Step 11: Using giveaway techniques to gather trust from the niche specialists

After a few weeks of starting the listing start sending your product to your niche specialists for free and ask them to review it on their websites and blogs. You can even run contests to give your products as a giveaway. With this method, you will get some positive reviews as a generous gesture.

Step 12: Send buyers a follow-up email asking for suggestions and feedback

Use third-party tracking cookies to remarket the visitors and after a successful order placement send the follow back emails to the consumers for feedback and suggestions. This is a good way to learn genuine feedback and usability remarks about your product. You can use these remarks to use them in your next-generation products.

Step 13: Use advertisements to generate sales

When organic reach is important for driving sales, you also need to depend on advertisements to improve your amazon search engine rank position. You can create automatic and manual advertisement campaigns to target your seed and long-tail keywords. You can crosscheck your sales and eliminate campaigns that are not working better.

Step 14: Dealing with defective pieces and return shipping

Some of the consumers will not be satisfied with your products for various reasons. It is natural and happens for every other seller. Take the Return products from the amazon warehouse and replace them with good products. Send those defective products to the supplier if they are in high quantity.

With this, we have completed a brief blueprint to one of the most profitable ways to earn money using the Amazon FBA program.

With this chapter, we have completed the book successfully and it is now in your hands to experiment with your sales using these tricks and techniques. Remember to believe in yourself!

You will do great with the Amazon FBA business. All the best!

Conclusion

Thank you for making it through to the end of *Amazon FBA*, let's hope it was informative and able to provide you with all the tools you need to achieve your goals whatever they may be.

The next step is to apply the knowledge you have learned in this book in the real world.

Finally, if you found this book useful in any way, a review on Amazon is always appreciated!

© **Copyright 2019 by Kiyo Richards - All rights reserved.**

This eBook is provided with the sole purpose of providing relevant information on a specific topic for which every reasonable effort has been made to ensure that it is both accurate and reasonable. Nevertheless, by purchasing this eBook you consent to the fact that the author, as well as the publisher, are in no way experts on the topics contained herein, regardless of any claims as such that may be made within. As such, any suggestions or recommendations that are made within are done so purely for entertainment value. It is recommended that you always consult a professional prior to undertaking any of the advice or techniques discussed within.

This is a legally binding declaration that is considered both valid and fair by both the Committee of Publishers Association and the American Bar Association and should be considered as legally binding within the United States.

The reproduction, transmission, and duplication of any of the content found herein, including any specific or extended information will be done as an illegal act regardless of the end form the information ultimately takes. This includes copied versions of the work both physical, digital and audio unless express consent of the Publisher is provided beforehand. Any additional rights reserved.

Furthermore, the information that can be found within the pages described forthwith shall be considered both accurate and truthful when it comes to the recounting of facts. As such, any use, correct or incorrect, of the provided information will render the Publisher free of responsibility as to the actions taken outside of their direct purview. Regardless, there are zero scenarios where the original author or the Publisher can be deemed liable in any fashion for any damages or hardships that may result from any of the information discussed herein.

Additionally, the information in the following pages is intended only for informational purposes and should thus be thought of as universal. As befitting its nature, it is presented without assurance regarding its prolonged validity or interim quality. Trademarks that are mentioned are done without written consent and can in no way be considered an endorsement from the trademark holder.

www.ingramcontent.com/pod-product-compliance
Lightning Source LLC
Chambersburg PA
CBHW032123250526
R18348000001B/R183480PG45466CBX00045B/9